The Way We Came

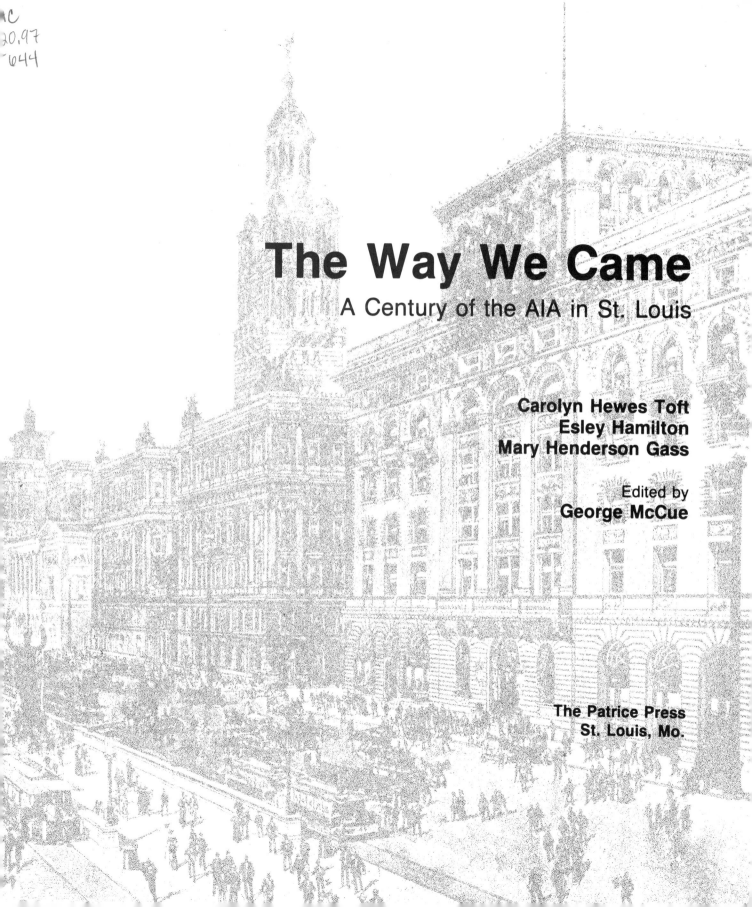

The Way We Came
A Century of the AIA in St. Louis

**Carolyn Hewes Toft
Esley Hamilton
Mary Henderson Gass**

Edited by
George McCue

**The Patrice Press
St. Louis, Mo.**

First Printing
December 1991

Library of Congress Cataloging in Publication Data

Toft, Carolyn Hewes.
  The way we came : a century of the AIA in St. Louis / Carolyn Hewes Toft, Esley Hamilton, Mary Henderson Gass : edited by George McCue.
      p.   cm.
  Includes index.
  ISBN 0-935284-93-1 (pbk) : $12.95
    1. American Institute of Architects.   Saint Louis Chapter. 2. Architecture—Missouri—Saint Louis. 3. Saint Louis (Mo.)—Buildings, structures, etc.   I. Hamilton, Esley, 1945- . II. Gass, Mary Henderson, 1946- . III. McCue, George. IV. Title.
  NA11.T64   1991
  720′.6077866—dc20   91-42168
                                                          CIP

Frontispiece: Vision of Twelfth Street as a corridor of stately buildings with curbed midway for streetcars, as proposed in 1894 by Craig McClure, A. M. Stewart, and Louis Mullgardt. At that time the removal of the old Lucas Market from Twelfth for a boulevard from Franklin Avenue to the Twelfth Street Bridge was under discussion.

American Architect, January 27, 1894.

Published by
The Patrice Press
1701 South Eighth Street
St. Louis MO 63104
Printed in the United States of America

To Betty Lou Custer, FAIA
whom we knew and loved as "BLC"
during her nineteen years as the Chapter's
Executive Secretary and Executive Vice-president

Union Station (1894) as background for AIA convention banner incorporating motif of Wainwright Building (1892). Both buildings were new showplaces at time of the 1895 national AIA convention, the first to be held in St. Louis, and both were in active new uses nearly a century later when the banner celebrated the city's fourth AIA convention in 1989.

Contents

St. Louisans Who Served as President, American Institute of Architects

William Scofield Eames, 1904-05 / 1916-17

John Lawrance Mauran, 1916-17

Ernest John Russell, 1933-35

George Edward Kassabaum, 1968

Foreword

The centennial of the St. Louis Chapter, American Institute of Architects, provides a unique occasion for reflecting on our past, present, and future. The wisdom in the remark that we can better tell where we are going if we know where we have been is part of the motivation for this book, *The Way We Came*.

Some of the Chapter's history will be as new to many members as to those of the public who, we hope, will also be interested, since this is a history of many aspects of St. Louis not dealt with in previous records.

St. Louis has changed since 1891 and so has this organization of architects in its service as a forum for talented and visionary professionals. During the same years of dedication to professional development, the AIA Chapter has grown in commitment to community service. I am confident that the Chapter will continue to be identified with these and other idealistic objectives in its second century.

It has been a special honor to serve as president during this milestone year, with its privilege of sharing these reflections on our first hundred years. We are proud of our tradition and eager to enlarge on our usefulness to our city, our state and region, and our nation.

Fred A Powers, AIA
President, St. Louis Chapter, AIA
1991

George Ingham Barnett, 1815-1898, the first professionally educated architect in St. Louis.

Introduction

In 1890, THE ST. LOUIS CHAPTER, American Institute of Architects, was established with twelve charter members and Pierce P. Furber as the first president. Or, the St. Louis Chapter was established in 1884 with eleven charter members and Henry G. Isaacs as the first president.

The passage of a century (or so) in the life of a distinguished organization evokes an elated sense of being. It has something to do with bare-fact survival, but a more earnest jubilation builds itself around the continuity of aspirations and ideals with which the organization has historically identified itself. Which are . . . ?

The blurring and scarcity of records leaves uncertainties as to what ideology was in place at the start, what was accrued, and as to who and what influenced early changes of direction. With much to account for and to commemorate, the St. Louis Chapter, AIA, commissioned this history in observance of the centennial dating from 1891, the year of the charter on its office wall, and one of the first research findings was that it could have observed another year of origin just as legitimately established and chartered seven years previously.

In common with other professional organizations, the Chapter emerged out of mixed priorities as to what it should be and do. Within a few years, assorted objectives were expressed from within impulsively organized peer-group institutes, associations, leagues, chapters, and clubs—regional and local.

Carolyn Hewes Toft has tracked their comings and goings by following often faint trails in documents, library archives, and nineteenth-century architectural magazines. She traces their mergers and splits, and their gravitations between club-by coziness and idealistic outreach. She finds that the St. Louis Chapter of 1884, having hung by a two-member thread for some months, became viable enough to survive through reorganization in 1890 and rechartering in 1891, and that born-again year is the one that is commemorated.

By their act of affiliation, the founders were responding to the need for a professional *esprit de corps* and for common ground where sometime competitors could unite in furtherance of their mutual interests. Chapter meetings provided forums for talks by eminent visitors, and sympathetic ears for the recounting of difficult experiences arising from acts of God and the sponsors of design competitions.

Early concerns of the AIA were to limit use of the term "architect" to those with professional education and experience in the arts of building and design, and to advocate state accreditation. Throughout the country, master builders (or "undertakers"), ordinary builders, contractors, carpenters, and draftsmen were identifying themselves as architects, accepting commissions for design and construction, and performing architectural services. Some performed badly, and some demonstrated remarkable aptitudes and intuitions in design and building, but lines of responsibility were haphazardly drawn.

When the Chapter was founded, St. Louis architecture was about midway between the French colonial cluster of plastered and whitewashed log houses on the riverfront and today's new skyline. Dwellings, warehouses, schools, and tall-spired churches testified to bold, energetic initiatives of the city's forerunner architects. Their designs were usually eclectic, with essences of historical styles blended into compositions that sometimes were incongruous. To an impressive extent, however, borrowed elements were applied with adroitness, sensitivity, vivacity, and sense of appropriateness that increasingly command respect from modern viewers. The early generations of de-facto architects were generally well educated but not technically trained.

A landmark event in St. Louis architec-

ture was the arrival in 1839 of a young Englishman, George Ingham Barnett, who had received professional training in London under Sir Thomas Hine. Barnett was at once enlisted to make a perspective drawing of the first unit of what is now the Old Courthouse, thus relieving an embarrassment of architect Henry Singleton.

Singleton had won the design competition with plans and elevations, but apparently—in common with most architects in this country at that time—had no training in perspective drawing. Barnett was to St. Louis what Benjamin Latrobe had been to Washington, D. C., thirty-six years earlier upon appointment by President Thomas Jefferson as Surveyor of Public Buildings and Architect of the Capitol. Each introduced technical architectural qualifications, happily combined with design talent, to his adopted city.

When St. Louis was growing into the nation's fourth largest city, specialized architectural knowledge became essential as construction grew in scale and complexity. Yet, when the American Institute of Architects was founded in 1857 there was not one school of architecture in the United States. The first American school of architecture was established at the Massachusetts Institute of Technology in 1866. Some of St. Louis's most respected practitioners in subsequent years were graduates of MIT, or of new architectural schools at Columbia or Cornell universities, with further training in Paris at the Ecole des Beaux Arts. Some early schools, including that of the University of Illinois, founded in 1870, were adjuncts of engineering departments. In 1890, Harvard established the first architectural school with orientation to design as art.

John Albury Bryan, pathfinder through St. Louis architectural history, related that the first degree in architecture awarded in St. Louis was to Harry Newington (who later practiced in New York City), in 1881 by the O'Fallon Polytechnic Institute. The school, affiliated with Washington University, offered art and design classes for manufacturing and mercantile applications. Later, the university's Manual Training School offered similar courses.

There is no indication that the Polytechnic actually had an architecture curriculum, and Newington's courses may have been custom-crafted. The university did not then offer the degree, but its St. Louis School of Art and Design, a special department under Halsey C. Ives, offered classes in drawing and design applicable to basic architectural training. In 1881 this school was moved into the Museum of Fine Arts building at Nineteenth and Locust streets given by merchant Wayman Crow and designed by Peabody & Stearns, of Boston. There, it shared space with the antecedent of the St. Louis Art Museum.

Esley Hamilton relates that the St. Louis Architectural Club, founded in 1894 by a group of young architects and draftsmen to further their education, functioned as an atelier. For some years—finally in its own quarters in a converted stable—the club offered the city's only classes in architectural design, construction, and allied arts on the professional level. Some members of the AIA Chapter joined the Architectural Club, delivered lectures, and in many cases provided on-the-job training in their firms. Several served as its president.

The Washington University School of Architecture, still the only one in Missouri, came into being at the downtown campus with three students in 1901 in association with the School of Engineering under Frederick M. Mann. On the new Cope & Stewardson campus, the schools jointly occupied Cupples Hall No. 1—with the Architectural Club conducting the university's evening classes in its own quarters for nearly two decades until the school moved to Givens Hall in 1933 and became free-standing.

One of the university's first graduates, Lawrence Hill of the class of 1901, returned in 1914 as professor of architectural history. The main focus of architectural history until well into the twentieth century was on classical and other academic design prototypes, and not many architects had, or would take, time to become interested in traditions of their own country and region, or in the vernaculars of their obscure or anonymous predecessors.

On his first visit to St. Louis in 1913, John Albury Bryan was immediately impressed by the character and variety of buildings that he saw in a long ride on a Delmar streetcar. In a memoir, he wrote admiringly of hotels, churches, an early movie theater, some Queen Anne flats, and a funeral parlor. Bryan worked under George E. Kessler, studied architecture at the Architectural Club and at Columbia University, became a design assistant with LaBeaume & Klein, and kept personal files of St. Louis buildings and their architects. For the national convention of the American Institute of Architects in St. Louis in 1928, the Architectural Club sponsored publication of his *Missouri's Contribution to American Architecture*, a copiously illustrated trailblazer book, still a prime reference.

Although the St. Louis Chapter had the expertise for useful guidance toward a public point of view in complex issues of urban design, architects tended to remain aloof from public discussion until the mid-twentieth century. Extravagantly grandiose and inherently unworkable City Beautiful schemes for the riverfront, put forth during decades following the Louisiana Purchase Exposition of 1904 and lavishly reported and illustrated in the newspapers, received no critical examination by the press or the Chapter. Most of them bore the stamp of the Chapter's most stalwart members. Their colleagues, usually with divergent opinions on almost any issue but neutral in public, were inhibited, too, by Institute strictures against questioning or challenging each other's projects outside their own circles.

Among other things that the Gateway Arch is a monument to is its commemoration of the Chapter's taking a leadership position in the public arena, with significant benefit to community and nation. In 1957, the Arch project had reached an almost terminal dead center, largely because of dreadful complexities of relocating railroad tracks that crossed the site. The Chapter president, Eugene Mackey, Jr., and Eric W. Smith, Jr., led their troops in support of getting the job done during months of crusading in public and private forums.

Mary Henderson Gass addresses the Chapter's modern era—the post-war years of land clearance, public housing, civic projects superimposed on the old downtown grid, and adaptive reuse of historic properties. During those years, the public became a party to nearly all major redevelopment—including private projects built with public funds or benefiting from

tax abatement; many also involved the taking of property from long-established use, which required at least public acquiescence, for radical redevelopment.

The questions were not just about architecture but about conceptions of land use and urban design more far-reaching than had previously challenged either the public or the professional experts. Never had the planners, architects, city administration, financial interests, and citizens of St. Louis been confronted with such perplexing choices, or with more possibilities of irreparable damage from well-meaning but badly informed and short-sighted decisions. Yet there they were, the suddenly urgent and politically sensitive problems of design and social priorities, especially in the downtown core.

In St. Louis, during the urban-renewal years of the early 1960s, redevelopers and funding agencies tended to have the last word in large-scale replacement planning and design. An authority charged with renewing bruised and broken parts of the city needed godly wisdom and vision, but those qualities usually were attached to hindsight. Unfortunately, the big complexes of elevator housing for low-income families and the Mill Creek Valley commercial redevelopment came too precipitately to serve as teaching examples of what not to do. Architecture could have served more effectively under a firm master plan with an uncommonly judicious mix of practical and idealistic aims, but some of the problems were beyond purely architectural solutions.

With hesitation at first, but with increasing readiness to contribute from its professional qualifications, the Chapter took two major steps toward educating the public in urban issues and itself in give-

and-take colloquy. Over several decades, it has organized and provided leadership for tours, talks, workshops, demonstrations, exhibitions, and publications, still being carried out and some widely emulated; and it has taken forthright positions on issues central to the public interest—the Gateway Mall, a hotel parking garage under Luther Ely Smith Park, and proposed removal of the remaining Cupples Station warehouses, among others. The Chapter assembled specialists for an influential study and report on the conservation of Forest Park.

In its annual Charrette, the Chapter has focused attention on long-postponed civic management by awarding prizes for studies and applicable concepts. These included design problems, such as a pedestrian bridge over Memorial Drive and I-70 to connect the Jefferson National Expansion Memorial and the Old Courthouse, and land-use problems, such as redevelopment of the industrial district south of the Memorial grounds.

Some proposals and declarations offered by the Chapter have swayed a course of action, and some have not (as yet), but they have contributed to understanding of the options. In its first century, the St. Louis Chapter, AIA, grew from a self-centered exclusive club to a potent influence on its community's environment. In its next century, the choices are likely to be harder, the options fewer, the improvements much more costly, and the social, political, and economic priorities more competitive.

The Chapter has established its place in the community, its authority, and its good will in defining implications of planning and design, and has made clear its commitment to the practical advantages of idealistic outcomes.

For this history, the St. Louis Chapter did not ask for, nor would the authors have been inclined to undertake in its behalf, a chronology of self-congratulation. The authors were given access to all available records and documents—some of which had overflowed into the garage of its executive vice-president, Betty Lou Custer—and were invited to tell it like it is. The account takes note of periods of inertia and wavering convictions, and it salutes the many substantial triumphs.

The name styles of architectural firms have changed through many decades from a general usage of "and" in the linkage of principals' names to the ampersand and to the ingenious devices of graphics designers. For the present purpose, the ampersand is arbitrarily imposed.

In 1957, when the St. Louis Chapter celebrated the centennial of the American Institute of Architects with a luncheon, the peppery and observant Louis LaBeaume delivered a reminiscence about architects and architecture in St. Louis, and their strengths and weaknesses, that the Chapter published in a booklet entitled *The Way We Came.* That title has been appropriated for this history of the Chapter with affectionate remembering of LaBeaume's prodding of his profession "to lead the way to that great new day of which we dream."

George McCue

Original seal, American Institute of Architects, commemorating its founding in New York City, 1857. Souvenir of the Twenty-ninth Annual Convention, American Institute of Architects, St. Louis, 1895.

I Haas & Co., St. Louis

I.

The Founding
(1884)1891-1918

By Carolyn Hewes Toft

St. Louis Architecture of the Late Nineteenth Century
Designs by Charter Members of the AIA Chapter

John William Nagel

Carved stone ornament of Romanesque Revival Cupples House, St. Louis University, 1890. Thomas B. Annan. Extant.

St. Louis Public Library

Romanesque Revival base of St. Louis Mercantile Library, Fifth (Broadway) & Locust, 1889. Henry G. Isaacs.

St. Louis Public Library

Roe Building, groping for a business aesthetic—Gothic details possibly carried over from church design, tower that erupts into the skyline, imported elements uneasily adapted and scaled; southwest corner Broadway and Pine, 1884. Francis D. Lee. Demolished.

Picturesque Teutonic medievalism in Anheuser-Busch brewery complex, 1885-91. Jungenfeld & Co. Extant, altered.

Maryville Academy of the Sacred Heart, institutional mix of Wren tower (the architect lectured on spires) and mansard roof above courses of arched windows, 1872, demolished 1973. James H. McNamara.

Pictorial St. Louis, Past and Present, Arista C. Shewey, 1892

St. Louis Cotton Exchange, window heads reflecting interest in polychrome materials and Renaissance punctuation, Main and Walnut, 1882, demolished 1940. H. William Kirchner (who also designed sixty schools for the Board of Education).

Pat Hays Baer, for Landmarks Association of St. Louis

Residence, 6015 West Cabanne Place, 1889, extant. Charles K. Ramsey.

1
The Twice-chartered Chapter

THE CHARTER hanging in the office of the St. Louis Chapter of the American Institute of Architects boasts the signatures of two very different giants in the profession: William Morris Hunt and Dankmar Adler. Hunt belonged to the patrician legacy of the East, Adler the robust diversity of the West. Together, they epitomized the newly forged, uneasy truce achieved within the Institute near the close of the nineteenth century. The date on the charter is December 5, 1891--an accident of history, or a memento to a local discord analogous to the wider contemporary antagonisms?

The St. Louis Chapter was actually organized on March 13, 1884, by a handful of prominent local practitioners: Thomas B. Annan, Henry G. Isaacs, Edmund Jungenfeld, H. William Kirchner, Francis D. Lee, and James H. McNamara. Most were recently admitted members of the national Institute; several had also been associated with the St. Louis Institute of Architects, an organization mentioned in local papers as early as 1875. (Incorporated in January 1870 with

George I. Barnett as president, the Institute's comprehehsive schedule of terms regulating local competitions was signed by twenty-seven members before publication in *The American Architect and Building News* in early 1881.) All had distinguished themselves during the post-Civil War building boom with designs for commercial blocks, banks, churches, public buildings, schools, and houses.

On March 15, 1884, Kirchner, secretary of the new Chapter, sent a letter to George C. Mason, secretary of the AIA, requesting official recognition of the Chapter. Mason's affirmative response was read by Isaacs, the Chapter's president, at the June meeting. A letter of congratulations had also been received from an enterprising editor of *Inland Architect,* a youthful and aggressive professional journal based in Chicago that would soon redirect the history of the Institute and its fledgling St. Louis Chapter.

Before the end of 1884, the list of St. Louis charter members was reopened to add Thomas H. Furlong, George I. Barnett, Ernst C. Janssen, Isaac S.

Taylor, and Otto J. Wilhelmi. Yet with Jungenfeld's death in December 1884, total membership stood at only ten in spite of repeated attempts to attract candidates.

Some potential members were busy with seditions instigated by *Inland Architect's* call for the creation of a pragmatic organization for "western" architects, a call that brought together more than 150 hearty souls in 1884 for a mid-November conclave in Chicago, where Mr. Nobody from Nowhere could rub shoulders with Burnham, Root, Adler, and Sullivan. Daniel Burnham was chosen temporary chairman of the gathering, but St. Louisan Charles E. Illsley emerged as the first president of the Western Association of Architects. St. Louis was selected for the 1885 convention.

Both of those politically shrewd moves were orchestrated in part by Charles K. Ramsey, soon to be associated with Adler & Sullivan, who advised Illsley to have an acceptance speech ready in Chicago. Although Ramsey was a member of the St. Louis Institute and a contemporary of the little band of Chapter members, he had not joined the Chapter. Neither had Illsley, even though both he and Ramsey were members of the national Institute.

Founders of this upstart challenge to the venerable New York-based AIA envisioned a free-wheeling, politically active, democratically run organization empowered by strong state-wide associations. Thus, the first chore for Illsley and Ramsey was to assemble a model Missouri Association before the 1885 convention. An organizational meeting held in St. Louis in March 1885 attracted more than fifty enthusiasts. Illsley, however, would have to turn part of his responsibility for the November convention over to other members of the local arrangements committee, inasmuch as the April 1885 issue of *Inland* announced that its editorial department had been strengthened by the addition of Illsley as an associate editor.

In contrast to Chicago architects who collectively had made an impression on the Eastern establishment and its mouthpiece, *The American Architect & Building News,* St. Louis's relatively conservative designers were virtually unknown. For them, Illsley's appointment to *Inland* offered unexpected opportunities for recognition in the official organ of the burgeoning Western Association.

Not surprisingly, *American Architect* began to take more note of St. Louis, not just the work of the first "foreign" firms in town such as Peabody & Stearns, but also designs from Isaacs, Ramsey, and others of more local reputation. But the publicity worked both ways. As more St. Louis projects appeared in the journals, more out-of-town firms entered local competitions and sent representatives to establish field offices. (William R. Hodges, the outspoken, influential critic for St. Louis's *Spectator,* had urged local architects in 1883 to abandon the passé "stone front, zinc cornice, iron column pseudo-classic cheap and nasty style" still prevalent in local residential architecture in favor of the "Modern" or be trampled by imported firms.)

The 1885 Western Association meeting was a triumph for the organization and its host city. Held on the heels of a sparsely attended AIA meeting at Nashville, the multitude in St. Louis was welcomed by James H. McNamara, charter member of the St. Louis AIA Chapter, long-time secretary of the old St. Louis Institute of

Architects, and local representative of the United States Supervising Architect's Office. William T. Sherman declined to address the delegates because of alleged stage fright, but happily met them informally at the banquet. Just about everybody who was anybody in St. Louis architecture was there, including most members of the local Chapter for whom the initiation fee was waived. Dankmar Adler, an early and ardent supporter of the Association, was elected president; Illsley became a director.

More than twenty states were represented including New York, which sent Louise Blanchard Bethune as one of its three representatives. After approving an impressive number of male candidates for membership, those assembled agreed unanimously with the board's strong recommendation that Mrs. Bethune be admitted to membership. The AIA would have to follow suit in 1888, a position in which it found itself with increasing regularity.

The most heated discussions at the convention revolved around the vexing problems with competitions, the need for an agreed-upon code of ethics and just who had the right to call himself an architect. A. J. Bloor, secretary of the national Institute and its official observer at the St. Louis meeting, remarked that the Western Association was grappling with twenty-seven-year-old issues. Precisely. The majority of its members found the Institute to be a timid little self-perpetuating bunch of "old fogies" incapable of taking decisive action. Upon Bloor's return to the East, editors of *American Architect* conceded that it might be time for the "older body to give authoritative expression" to some of the more pressing problems.

The journal's overt paternalism merely

reflected the philosophy of a conservative Institute governed like a gentlemen's club with two very different categories of "active" members: Fellows and Associates. The Western Association, on the other hand, had adopted a brash constitution admitting only one class of active members: Fellows. This egalitarian approach plus lower fees and more ferment assured support for the Missouri State Association from St. Louis architects.

By 1887, when talk of consolidation preoccupied both the national Institute and the national Association, the St. Louis AIA Chapter was almost nonexistent. All living charter members had joined the Missouri Association save President Henry G. Isaacs and Secretary H. William Kirchner who, along with the national Institute itself, kept up the pretense of a functioning St. Louis Chapter.

Given the political climate within the profession, the Institute's decision to go to Chicago for its 1887 meeting was not undertaken lightly. After considerable debate at the convention about the wisdom of a merger with the Western Association, a committee headed by Daniel Burnham (an esteemed member of both groups) was appointed to bring a definitive report to the next meeting. That gathering, held in Buffalo in 1888, turned into a boisterous floor fight unheard of in the previous annals of the outwardly decorous AIA. At its conclusion, Burnham's candidacy for Institute president had been derailed, but nothing had been settled about the merger.

In February 1889 a joint committee from the Institute and the Association met for three days, then emerged with a consolidation constitution and bylaws setting forth the agreed-upon definition of an ar-

Souvenir, Twenty-ninth Convention, 1895

Store building, Ninth and Washington, 1887. Alfred F. Rosenheim.

chitect: ". . . a professional person whose occupation consists in originating and supplying artistic and scientific data, primarily to and in connection with the construction of buildings, their appurtenances and decorations, in supervising the operation of contractors therefor and in preparing contracts between the proprietor and contractors thereof."

The constitution included two key compromises. Since the AIA was cited in considerable case law in the United States, the Institute's name would be carried forward as the name of the new organization; all current members of both organizations were to be admitted as Fellows. Respec-

tive secretaries mailed the documents to all members for a letter vote on consolidation.

The vote in favor of merger was overwhelming from both groups, but the August 1889 issue of *Inland* complained that the secretary of the Institute was stalling plans for a joint reorganization convention. Finally, both parties agreed to hold the meeting in Cincinnati. *The American Architect,* in a rare display of outright petulance, predicted an attendance of about twenty-five. Four times that number actually participated. St. Louis sent seven: Louis C. Bulkley, Charles C. Hellmers, Illsley (who would be elected a director), McNamara (who delivered a paper on domes and towers), Ramsey, and Alfred F. Rosenheim. After a final bit of mistrustful parliamentary procedure, the Institute bravely prepared itself for the invasion of hordes of Western Association members.

Richard Morris Hunt, generously elected president given his impassioned speech in opposition to merger the year before, gave an emotional address followed by reports from various Institute chapters presented by Secretary Bloor. Included among chapters reporting what seemed to "indicate a satisfactory condition of interest and activity on the part of the members" was St. Louis. Clearly, not all architects in St. Louis concurred.

Pierce P. Furber, who had been sent to St. Louis by Peabody & Stearns of Boston, quickly shed his Eastern cloak and joined the Missouri Association in late 1886. An affable young man who apparently thrived on organizations, Furber sent modest letters to *American Architect* and *Inland Architect* in the spring of 1889: "I enclose a copy of the constitution and

13 | The Twice-chartered Chapter

bylaws of the Architects' Club in St. Louis which has just been formed with a membership of fifteen. Officers are: President, P. P. Furber; Secretary, L. C. Bulkley; Treasurer, A. F. Rosenheim. The committee thought you might like to know that St. Louis was trying to keep up with the procession.''

This short-lived organization was a preliminary challenge to the existing local chapter, not a sketch club for draftsmen. Furber's name appeared in *Inland* a few months later as a judge at the first annual meeting of the St. Louis Architectural League—the first of several attempts to establish a draftsmen's club.

In the March 29, 1890, *American Architect,* one finds yet another communique from St. Louis: "Dear Sirs, will you kindly announce in your next issue that there has been organized in this city a St. Louis Chapter with the following officers and members: President, P. P. Furber; Vice-President, James H. McNamara; Secretary, A. F. Rosenheim; Treasurer, Charles K. Ramsey. Associates: T. C. Link, J. Beattie, T. B. Annan, T. J. Furlong, W. S. Eames, T. C. Young, C. W. Clark, K. Tully. Sincerely, A. F. Rosenheim, Secretary.''

Furber would have only a brief tenure as president of the resuscitated St. Louis Chapter. The Chapter report filed with the Institute at its 1890 convention in Washington, D. C., in late October mentions that the Chapter had held seven meetings, and states that William S. Eames had just been elected president. (Link became vice-president; Ramsey and Rosenheim retained their offices.)

Eames, Link, and Rosenheim were among the 104 members attending the Institute's twenty-fourth annual convention.

(*Inland* insisted for a spell that the convention should rightfully be called the second, but eventually gave up.) Illness kept President Hunt from Washington, so it was impossible for the secretary to obtain his signature on the charters of the chapters that had reorganized since the merger. (The new charters were regarded as souvenirs of that event; the old charters were still considered valid.) Finally, in January 1891, the Institute's board authorized secretary Dankmar Adler to issue those charters on his own. The St. Louis charter is dated December 5, 1891.

The Chapter has almost no records before 1920, so it is impossible to divine just what might have happened to the first incarnation of the St. Louis Chapter, but it is clear that one existed. Minutes in Kirchner's hand from the initial year can be found at the Missouri Historical Society; a history of the Institute prepared for the 1890 convention by the AIA's secretary, A. J. Bloor, states that the St. Louis Chapter was organized in 1884; so does *The A.I.A.'s First Hundred Years,* published by the Institute in 1957.

Even more tantalizing is a series of letters from 1900 written by Glenn Brown, secretary of the Institute, to the Chapter and a 1922 letter from Kirchner to the Chapter's membership chairman. Brown's first note is dated February 8, 1900: "I have a letter from Mr. W. H. Kirchner who is a member of the American Institute of Architects, and he feels that he has been, to a certain extent, slighted in not being asked to become a member of the St. Louis Chapter. . . . He informs me that he assisted in the organization of the Chapter in 1884. If there is no reason why he should not be a member of your Chapter, will you be kind enough to take steps to see that he may become one?'' The Chapter's response has disappeared. Brown's longer letter of February 26 recited the early history of the Chapter (charter issued April 16, 1884, etc.) and again urged that Kirchner be brought back in without the formality of reelection. Obviously, the Chapter balked. In Brown's final communique, he agreed to notify Kirchner that the Chapter could and would impose requirements.

Twenty-two years later, Kirchner responded to what must have been a random letter looking for new Chapter members among past Fellows of the national Institute. ''I never regretted anything more than my resignation from the Institute, or to put it differently, I have never regretted anything more than to be obliged to resign. When the St. Louis Chapter opened its doors to men whose sole ambition was to ''get the job,'' I was out of the running. *De mortuis nil nisi bene* [sic]. . . .''

Souvenir, Twenty-ninth Convention, 1895

City Hall, council chamber detail, mantel and portion of north wall, 1895, architect George R. Mann. (Not built; interior design awarded to Weber & Groves in 1903.)

2
The Code and the Competitions

WITH NATIONAL CONSOLIDATION an accomplished fact came a reshuffling of regional affiliations. In a few years the majority of St. Louis architects would no longer support the once-essential Missouri Chapter, née association, but at the close of 1890 at least twenty-six of them still belonged. The St. Louis Chapter could claim only twelve members. Theodore C. Link, president of the state group, and Illsley were particularly committed to preserving a state-wide organization to advocate registration legislation dear to the heart of the Association.

"We must work toward legal status for the profession. In St. Louis, architects are taxed the same as tradesmen! If architects will just look at the legal situation, and even their social status, compared with two inferior professions, law and medicine, they will see that more important than fees, more important than monuments of their skill is the securing of a legal status which will declare architecture to be a profession and not a Trade." Those words in *Inland* were undoubtedly written by Illsley, St. Louis's first member of the Institute's board of directors.

Throughout his many years as editor with *Inland*, Illsley admonished the profession to demand respect by supporting registration, avoiding competitions, and abiding by adopted fee schedules. Not shy, Illsley took on the *New York Herald* over his own signature in a tightly controlled response of outrage to that paper's contention, repeated in the *St. Louis Globe-Democrat,* that scores of architects, including at least ten in St. Louis, made more than $100,000 per year. "Will the *Herald* name to me a single architect in St. Louis, who at any time derived from his practice a revenue of $100,000 per annum, or of half that amount?" No response was forthcoming. Richard Morris Hunt's work for "swell" clients in baronial Newport notwithstanding, Illsley's fear that the article was likely "to create public odium against a severely over-worked and under-paid profession" had merit.

Even with the stipulation that the school board architect in St. Louis could take no outside work, competing candidates from

Union Station, private dining room, 1894. Theodore C. Link.

the Chapter vied for the position with a yearly salary of $3,000. Even with a competition for Union Station offering just half the Institute's adopted fee for the winning architect, only four invited firms (Shepley, Rutan & Coolidge; Peabody, Stearns & Furber; S. S. Beman, and Eames & Young) refused to compete on those terms. Even with an agreed-upon fee for the final design and superintending of the other big commission in town, the new City Hall, architect George R. Mann (who joined the Chapter in 1891) would be subjected to appalling countermands, constant political interference, and

"downright insolence" from his multi-headed client.

New members from 1891 in addition to Mann (who had moved to St. Louis in a futile attempt to control the City Hall job) included Charles F. May, William B. Ittner, Ernst C. Janssen, George U. Heimburger, and Edward A. Cameron (partner with Link in the successful Union Station design), plus Professor Halsey C. Ives, the Chapter's first honorary member. Ives would also become St. Louis's first honorary member of the Institute.

Thirty-three-year-old Thomas C. Young was elected president for the 1891-92 term; McNamara, a veteran of twenty years of architects' meetings, returned as vice-president. Information could be gleaned about only one meeting in 1891, an exemplary session that brought Chapter and Sketch Club members together to hear a paper by McNamara on St. Louis spires, after which criticisms were presented on the five best Sketch Club entries for a Gothic spire to complete Christ Church Cathedral.

St. Louis's 1891 report to the convention cited the adoption of a code of ethics governing its membership as the year's most important effort. Seven members took the train trip to Boston where both Furber and Eames, Chapter past presidents, were nominated for three-year director terms. Only Eames won. He and Illsley, who still had a year to serve, would spend a good deal of time and money traveling to 1892 board meetings in New York along with trying to attend Congressional hearings on the profession's perennial battle over the operations of the Supervising Architect's Office in the U. S. Department of the Treasury.

With Furber's election to a three-year

director's term at the Chicago convention in October 1892, St. Louis maintained its enviable two-person representation on the national governing body. Chapter President Young's annual report contained a sharp response to the Institute's circular letter of inquiry about the need for state chapters. After allowing the benefits of state organizations in geographically small eastern states, Young attacked the concept: ". . . in western states with two or more cities of metropolitan proportions . . . state membership would be composed mostly of malcontents and individuals whose personal or professional standing excludes them from participation in local Chapters."

Indeed, the Chapter could not bring participants it desired into the fold, and proposed a resolution intent on forcing members of the Institute living in a town or city with an established chapter to become members. On the positive side, the Chapter reported tremendous response to its first annual exhibit of architectural drawings. Held in February at the Museum of Fine Arts, then at Nineteenth and Locust streets, in the Peabody & Stearns building given to Washington University by Wayman Crow, the exhibit, not limited to works by St. Louisans, attracted more than three thousand viewers in two weeks.

Young was reelected president for the 1892-93 term; a beleaguered George R. Mann assumed the office of vice-president. The Institute's executive committee met in Washington in mid-January of 1893 with Eames and Furber in attendance in the vain hope that the Institute could arrange for them to testify about the Supervising Architect's Office before a congressional committee. A matter about which there had never been any disagreement between the Institute and the Association, the monopoly of the Supervising Architect's Office in federal design projects was a wearisome subject occupying considerable space in journals for almost two decades. In an era of unprecedented federal building throughout the country, the turn-of-the-century Institute was especially keen on reforms that would give its members opportunities to compete. The Tarsney Act, which provided for limited competitions and was passed before the 1893 AIA convention in Chicago, was a hollow victory, because its power was at the discretion of a Secretary of the Treasury who would not comply.

Routine AIA convention business in Chicago was overshadowed by the excitement and tension of the Columbian Exposition. Local scribes and practitioners reacted to criticisms of the fair in the eastern press with rhapsodic excesses of self-congratulation: ". . . the general view of the grand basin and south lagoon has no equal in architectural composition on the face of the earth. . . ."

The sober 1893 Chapter report, filed in July for the October convention, reported four new active members and the addition of a new honorary member—retired architect George I. Barnett. Tragically, Furber had died of a virulent case of diphtheria just weeks after his fortieth birthday. (His demise was the end of Peabody & Stearns in St. Louis.) The convention elected Rosenheim to fill out the last two years of Furber's term on the board.

It must have given the Chapter's three newest members (Craig McClure, Louis Mullgardt, and A. M. Stewart) great satisfaction to see *American Architect* run a

Chicago's Columbian Exposition of 1893 inspired grand and grandiose civic design visions in many cities, including St. Louis. The Market House competition, sponsored by the Architectural Club in 1893, attracted the confection below by Louis C. Mullgardt—who went on to design for the San Francisco-Panama Pacific Exposition,

1915. The Market House competition shown above is by William B. Ittner. It joined classical porticos and a Renaissance clock tower in a scheme with vaulted cross aisles particularly disliked by Robert S. Peabody of Peabody & Stearns, who juried the competition.

Cupples Station warehouse No. 5, Ninth and Spruce, c.1893. Eames & Young.

full-page plate in early 1894 of their monumental scheme for the former Lucas Market expanse on Twelfth Street between Market and St. Charles. The journal also reported ''civic interest'' in purchasing two blocks of property opposite Union Station (still under construction) to create an open square. Later in the year came word that Julius Pitzman, St. Louis's foremost civil engineer and new honorary member of the Chapter, had proposed a $2 million street improvement plan that included widening Market Street from Twelfth Street to Jefferson Avenue.

All this and more appeared in *American Architect's* two-year run of ''Letters from St. Louis.'' Newsy but highly opinionated, the ''Letters'' sound a lot like the Chapter's most successful but prickly author, Charles E. Illsley: ''Progress is often hampered these days in St. Louis by people who have never been known to make the world any better off by their presence in it.'' Protective of the work of St. Louis architects, critical of that by ''foreign'' designers (especially Adler &

Sullivan), the anonymous chronicler defined the horizons of a corrupt city government to readers throughout the country.

The terse Chapter report to the convention of 1894 merely listed the number of members (thirty-five, with seventeen regular, twelve associates, and six honorary) and recorded an unusually large number of meetings. Not mentioned were the new officers: elder statesman Thomas B. Annan, president, balanced by thirty-year-old William B. Ittner, vice-president.

Caspar Boisselier, one of the three new members, accompanied seven other representatives to the 1899 convention in New York City where Eames (elected second vice-president) became the first Chapter member to rise to the Institute's executive committee. Link, elected to his first term on the board, found himself on the Education and Libraries Committee, along with luminaries such as William Le Baron Jenney and Cass Gilbert. The choice for the 1895 meeting was St. Louis, the farthest west the Institute had yet ventured.

But not all was well in St. Louis as the city prepared for the honor. *American Architect* proclaimed it as among the worst-managed in the country. Although Union Station was opened in September to boosterism worthy of Chicago, the most obvious physical evidence of an inept government was impossible to conceal—City Hall. ''Whenever a new municipal or other public building is to be erected in this country, intelligent people have learned to expect that officers elected and appointed to care for its erection will distinguish themselves by the adroit way in which they will delay its completion, entangle its construction and increase its cost regardless of all legal restrictions. The new City Hall at St. Louis . . . now stands as an empty skeleton, the sport of the elements while a 'thorough investigation' is being conducted by city officials.'' Local wags suggested that the two niches above the main entrance should be reserved for statues of ''our virtuous mayor and incorruptible president of the City Council.''

The convention was opened with a few pithy remarks by Mayor Cyrus P. Walbridge at a formal reception on the ground floor of the Museum of Fine Arts. Then guests ascended to the galleries to open an exhibition organized jointly by the St. Louis Architectural Club and the Chapter. Sessions were called to order by President Daniel Burnham the next day at the leisurely hour of 11 A.M. The scene was the banquet hall of the new St. Nicholas Hotel, an Adler & Sullivan project where the architects were lodged in rooms without bath for $1.50 to $2. (Rooms with bath ran from $2.50 to $4.) After expressing the Institute's sorrow on the losses of James Renwick and Richard Morris Hunt, Burnham suggested that more than one chapter be allowed in a single geographic area. Young spoke at length against that proposal when it was offered later as an amendment to the bylaws.

Illsley's paper on one of his favorite subjects, ''Cooperation Versus Competition,'' met with resounding applause,and other parts of the program seem to have engendered a mood of uplift. As reported in *Inland,* probably by Illsley again: ''The Convention of '95 will long be notable for the profuse and appropriate entertainment programs furnished by the local Chapter; Professor Johnson's tests of the strength of

American timber, the carriage rides and lunches, the visit to Hydraulic Press Brick and other proprietors of wholesale establishments . . . it was perhaps a greater surprise for the Eastern visitors to drive through parks which environ the city . . . and if the greatest brewery in the world was visited and some of its product absorbed, the delegates could not be blamed for subsequent enthusiasm.''

The Chapter report to the convention was one breathless sentence: ''The St. Louis Chapter has held ten meetings, with supper, and has been diligently at work preparing for this Convention.'' No officers were named nor was a count of members included. Happily, an issue of *Carpentry & Building* recorded the dramatic shift in leadership for 1895-96 with new faces in three of the four positions: president, Robert W. Walsh; vice-president, Louis Mullgardt; treasurer, John L. Wees. Rosenheim was retained as secretary. (Additional information is contained in a tiny publication from January 1896 in the Chapter archives: the *Revised Constitution and Bylaws* with an appended list of twenty-five regular, six associate, and six honorary members.)

In February 1896 the Chapter addressed a concern shared by many around the country—that gloom and chills in downtown corridors might ensue as new technology sent skyscrapers soaring to unheard-of heights. The Chapter demonstrated the seriousness of its concern by spending five hours discussing a draft ordinance prepared by Professor Ives that would limit the height of new buildings. With disagreements resolved by amendments, the prolonged meeting produced a final draft to be presented to the City Council with the Chapter's full support.

Too late to affect the sixteen-story "705 Olive" and Chemical buildings, (skyscrapers by Chicago firms), the restriction would affect Eames & Young's first and best skyscraper—the twelve-story Lincoln Trust (later Title Guaranty) Building.

The Institute's board of directors also met in February with Link, but not Eames, in attendance. Along with the tiresome topic of the Supervising Architect was a tempting proposal from the publishers of the "St. Louis Convention Souvenir" to prepare without cost to the Institute a handsome two-volume history of the Institute including copy written by prominent members of the profession, biographies, and photos of past and present members. (The researcher's pulse quickens at the possibility that this was approved and that somewhere a copy exists. Not so.) The second volume would have featured prominent buildings and contractors; it was they who would pay. Unprofessional. The Institute had already decreed that permitting one's name or photo to accompany a builder's or manufacturer's advertisement was unseemly. That notion was observed more in the breach than in the compliance.

After a year of leadership by newcomers, the Chapter elected Charles K. Ramsey to its highest office for the 1896-97 term. An important figure in professional politics with a very successful practice, Ramsey so far has been of interest to scholars not for his own contributions but rather for his coup in associating with Adler & Sullivan. The Chapter's membership total of twenty-six practicing architects had not changed since the previous year; two members had resigned but two had been elected. Eames and Link were the only representatives at the

1896 convention in Nashville. Attendance in general was meager, prompting *American Architect* to promote an amendment that future meetings be held at a constant location and delegates be assigned from each Chapter based on the number of Institute members.

The competition of note in St. Louis in 1896, a new home for the prestigious St. Louis Club, was won by Friedlander & Dillon of New York, who beat Eames & Young; Shepley, Rutan & Coolidge, and an intrepid new Chapter member, Montrose P. McArdle. George R. Mann was another Chapter member who continued to play the competition lotteries. After coming in second behind Cass Gilbert in a protracted, disagreeable competition for the Minnesota State Capitol, Mann won first prize for his Montana statehouse.

Nationally, the profession scored two long-awaited victories. The first license law in the country was passed in Illinois and President McKinley appointed a Secretary of the Treasury who opened federal architecture to limited competitions. A scant thirty-one projects over the next fifteen years actually became available. The local firm to reap the greatest rewards was Eames & Young.

In late September 1897 the Chapter reelected Ramsey; McArdle vaulted to vice-president; Ittner returned as treasurer; Rosenheim remained the scribe. Apparently nineteenth-century AIA conventions were only for the gents—special mention was made in *Inland* about Mrs. Ittner's appearance with her husband and Link in Detroit for the convention at the Cadillac Hotel. The Chapter's report for 1897 showed a loss of one member. In February of the following year, Ittner was elected president of the St. Louis Architec-

Charles K. Ramsey, as caricatured in a book of cartoons and caricatures, St. Louisans as We See 'em. *(St. Louis, A Noble, c.1905) Ramsey became an associate of Adler & Sullivan in their St. Louis projects.*

tural Club, an assignment that was something of an anomaly for a Chapter officer.

One of several attempts to sustain a local sketch club was reported in *Inland* in 1889 when its editor came to town to describe the workings of the Chicago club to the nascent St. Louis Architectural League. Subsequently, the League held exhibits, sponsored competitions, and provided entertainments, but in March 1891 *Inland* editorialized: "After a number of unsuccessful efforts to establish an architectural sketch club, the draftsmen have at a last a plan that may prove successful. All have failed to date because of lack of interest in the work and on account of unsociability of the members."

The new plan was simply to place everything in the hands of three advisers who would furnish entertainment, prepare competitions, and choose judges for the newly named St. Louis Architectural Club. The first competition was the aforementioned program to add a spire to Christ Church Cathedral; a more ambitious competition for a new market house was held in 1893. Juried by Robert S. Peabody, the entries appeared in *American Architect* along with Peabody's criticisms directing the competitors to further study of "old monuments" rather than attempting to be modern, original, or American.

Even with Furber and John L. Wees as

advisers, the Club's efforts lapsed. Next came the "Base Ball Society," replaced in October 1894 by the formation of the Architectural Sketch Club at a large meeting in George R. Mann's temporary office next to the City Hall job. Rockwell M. Milligan was elected president, and letters were read from absent supporters, including Illsley, who wished to be placed on the rolls. Almost sixty signed up that night.

In 1896, the club returned to the old name, the St. Louis Architectural Club, and adopted a new constitution under which it confined itself to the study of architecture and the allied arts. Credit for the emphasis on education may be due Albert Guissart, a talented young Frenchman who came to St. Louis at the time of the City Hall competition and served the Club as "the preceptor of those young men who were working to better their professional education." Obviously, the Club was not meant to compete with the Chapter, but it did. Chapter President Thomas C. Young's report to the 1898 convention in Washington, D. C., was bleak: Two regular members and one associate had resigned, and the memberships of three regulars and one associate had lapsed.

Even though Chapter membership was stagnant, St. Louis still retained enough Institute members to merit four official delegates—John L. Mauran, Louis Mullgardt, A. F. Rosenheim, and newly-elected president William B. Ittner—to the 1899 convention in Pittsburgh. William S. Eames and Thomas C. Young went as observers. Eames returned as first vice-president, and Henry Van Brunt of Kansas City was elected Missouri's first president as the Institute entered another

Souvenir, Twenty-ninth Convention, 1895

Planters Hotel, for many years the city's most popular inn, Fourth Street, between Chestnut and Pine, 1894. (Demolished.) Isaac S. Taylor. The Old Courthouse is at left and the corner tower of the Roe Building is a block away, in the right background.

period of competition from a rival organization. All in all, 1899 had been an unsettling year. The St. Louis Chapter could count only twenty-four regular and three associate members; the St. Louis Architectural Club had enlisted 130 recruits! The phenomenon was not unique.

Initiated by the Chicago Sketch Club, the first assembly of architectural clubs convened in Cleveland in the summer of 1899. Papers were read, innocent discussions held, and agreements reached about lending lantern slides, sharing exceptional lectures, and sponsoring traveling exhibi-

tions. When it was all over, the Architectural League of America had been born. The League's stated attitude toward the Institute was one of deference and respect. *Inland,* however, trumpeted the news as "the most notable event in the architectural history of this country since the revival of the AIA by its consolidation with the Western Association."

Comparison with the Association was apt. Fifteen years had passed since its inception, ten since its members had been folded into the Institute. In that decade, professional training had been trans-

formed. Locally, George I. Barnett's death at age 84 in 1898 tolled the end of an era when hopefuls depended on apprenticeships with established practitioners. While the fortunate might manage to acquire some independent travel and study in Europe, the best possible nineteenth-century pedigree listed a diploma from the Ecole des Beaux Arts in Paris. But George B. Post, in his presidential address to the 1899 convention, served notice that France was going out of fashion: ". . . the splendid hospitality of the Ecole des Beaux Arts is no longer essential to the complete equipment of American Architects. Graduates of our own schools are becoming evident, making good their place in the ranks."

To codify its conversion to higher education, the Institute decided that all candidates for membership except those with degrees from acceptable schools of architecture would be subject to examination as of 1901. The University of Illinois, offering the only program close to St. Louis, was not on the approved list. Although Massachusetts Institute of Technology (the oldest American school of architecture) held entrance exams in St. Louis and

Landmarks Association of St. Louis

Lincoln Trust Building (later Title Guaranty), 1898, southwest corner of Seventh and Chestnut streets. (Demolished.) Eames & Young.

Landmarks Association of St. Louis

Attic story windows of the Lincoln Trust/Title Guaranty were set deep within lush ornamentation of maidens, heads, scrolls, and garlands executed by the Winkle Terra Cotta Company.

25 | The Code and the Competitions

William S. Eames, in St. Louisans as We See 'em.

nineteen other locations, the sole place in Missouri where draftsmen had an opportunity for continuing education was the St. Louis Architectural Club.

An anonymous voice from the old guard stated objections that a few still harbored to unbridled higher education: "A draftsman must have a year or more of practice under the supervision of a practicing architect before taking any college courses or he is apt to be hampered with mannerisms or an undue belief in his personal ability." Worse yet, engineers were becoming better educated all the time. How long would they be willing to work in subordination to the architect? The profession needed fewer draftsmen "who think they are artistic" and more draftsmen paying attention to construction details.

The social order in architecture had already changed. Exceptional draftsmen could give a firm the edge in competitions; crafty draftsmen had become partners in design. The second annual meeting of the Architectural League of America attracted five St. Louisans, including two of the most superb delineators, Oscar Enders and Edward G. Garden. Sullivan, the League's spiritual muse, and Frank Lloyd Wright attended from Chicago. Ittner was defeated for League president by another Chicagoan, but the St. Louis Chapter president was honored as one of the two delegates chosen to represent the League at the International Congress of Architects' meeting later that summer in Paris. Closer to home, Ittner finally saw one of his innovative designs for the Board of Education published.

Reelected by his Chapter for the 1900 term, President Ittner took a nine-man

delegation to the next convention in Washington, D. C. This, the thirty-fourth annual meeting, signalled a new focus for the national body. Having left its ancestral roots in New York City in 1898 for the historic Octagon House in Washington, the Institute was in an admirable position to influence national affairs. Preparations for the convention were entrusted to two District notables, Glenn Brown and J. C. Hornblower, and to William S. Eames, who thus earned appointments to Institute committees charged with pursuing two vital topics: a threatened defacement of the White House and the urgent need for an Arts Commission to plan and review development in the District. A motion by Ittner at the convention for the Institute to confer with the League on mutual points of interest was shuttled to the Board of Directors.

Ittner, wearing his other hat, gave one of the St. Louis papers at the April 1901 League meeting in Philadelphia. His topic, preparations for the Louisiana Purchase Exposition (planned for 1903 but held in 1904), had just received a mention in *Inland* which credited Daniel Burnham with the success of the Chicago Fair and commended local organizers for selecting a similar personality, Isaac S. Taylor, to head operations in St. Louis. Taylor and Burnham, who resembled each other in size, both possessed the "forceful, indomitable, overpowering will to carry all before them and *compel* success."

The Exposition was also discussed at the December 1901 AIA convention in Buffalo. Chapter president Eames's proposal that the Institute attempt to attract the International Congress for a concurrent meeting occasioned a barb from *American Architect* that questioned the desire of foreign visitors to come to St. Louis, given stories about "Tammany tigers, red-skins, squaws, buffalos and other objectionable animals." Theirs was the first volley in what would become a barrage of condescending remarks about the city and its Fair. By 1904, however, some of the city's most blatant problems were at least identified thanks to the 1901 election of Mayor Rolla Wells.

Wells had promised voters a "New St. Louis," a better-run and more beautiful city in time for the Fair. In June 1902 he asked the Chapter to name a committee to assist in the inspection and construction of public improvements. The Chapter selected T. C. Young, M. P. McArdle, A. B. Groves, J. L. Mauran, R. M. Milligan, and Ittner. Ittner, Young, and Mauran, along with James P. Jamieson and Emmanuel L. Masqueray, also sat on a committee to select the recipient of a $1,000 travel scholarship at the new course in architecture at Washington University. Directed by Frederick M. Mann, the program—divided into construction, practice, draftsmanship, architectural design, and history—opened its doors to three candidates for a B. S. in Architectural Engineering in the fall of 1901. (The department remained under the direction of Professor Mann, B. S. and M. S. from MIT, until 1910.)

The University could also offer an Architects Diplôme par la Gouvernement through its association with the St. Louis Architectural Club and the Beaux Arts Society in New York. By 1905, when the School of Engineering moved into Cupples Hall on the new campus, eleven students were enrolled in the regular program. Twice that number attended evening ateliers at the Club led by St. Louis-born,

Ecole-trained Louis C. Spiering. Chapter presidents in those intervening years included John L. Mauran (1902-03) and Theodore C. Link (1904-05). Ittner became president of the American League of Architects at its meeting in St. Louis in 1903. In 1904, Eames became the first St. Louis member of the profession elected president of the Institute.

In addition to a fair that actually made a profit, early twentieth-century St. Louis, with presidents of both national organizations, may have enjoyed the most harmonious relationship among architects throughout the country. Members of the Chapter participated in the Club; Washington University faculty supported both organizations, and city fathers encouraged professional participation in government. In November 1904, a committee of three Chapter members, Mauran, Eames, and Groves, handed Mayor Wells a document that was "persuasive, attractively printed and beautifully illustrated."

But *The Report of the Public Buildings Commission* was not a dreamy vision of the City Beautiful—it was an indictment. 'Your commission is a unit in pronouncing the present conditions intolerable, placing the responsibility for correcting these evils where it belongs, upon the citizens themselves, and calling upon them to redeem the fair name of the city and relieve their consciences. . . ." After deplorable conditions were outlined, the report demanded massive outlays of public monies for the Insane Asylum, the Female Hospital, the Poor House, the House of Refuge, the Work House, the City Hospital, the Public Market, the Four Courts, and the City Jail. The report also offered two different schemes for a public

Thomas C. Young, with crown as mayor of Webster Groves (his term, 1901-04) in St. Louisans as We See 'em.

buildings grouping. Much of this Chapter work would reappear in the Civic League City Plan of 1907.

The announcement in 1904 that Eames & Young had won the competition for the Federal Custom House in San Francisco created a stir in West Coast newspapers, but President Eames was busy with arrangements for the thirty-eighth annual AIA convention in Washington, D. C. Pushed into January of 1905, the gathering opened with Eames beating a challenge for a second term from a faction that could muster no more than twelve votes for Robert Peabody, and closed with a banquet attended by President Theodore Roosevelt, the mayor of greater New York City, several Supreme Court justices, and barons such as J. Pierpont Morgan. Eames, as president of the Institute, gave a toast to the President of the United States.

With the resignation of Louise Bethune in 1905, the Institute lost its sole female member. Women, however, were in the forefront of the Municipal Reform movement. Some of them had backgrounds in art and art history, and a few had entered architectural programs in this country. The Ecole des Beaux Arts did not admit women. Women were not allowed at sessions of the International Congress, although they could grace the accompanying excursions and social events.

American Architect, not a measure of progressive thought, amused itself with correspondence from a lady who thought that since a house means so much more to a woman than it does to a man, women should be encouraged to study seriously the principles of architectural proportions, the proper use of detail, and other such elements of design. ''We cannot say that we are very sanguine as to the value of any more feminine assistance in house planning than that which is already available. . . .''

The first woman to graduate from Washington University School of Architecture was Henrietta May Steinmesch, class of 1916, who managed to have a fascinating career ''wandering through a maze of architecture, city planning, display design, interior design, and work for Uncle Sam. . . . If I could write, I'd tell the story of the excuses offered me for not hiring a woman architect! One requirement: a good sense of humor.''

For years, the Institute had tried to divert members from competitions in contravention of professional standards first enumerated by the Western Association. Debate at the 1905 convention actually put an Institute member on trial for participating in a flawed competition, although many participants thought an even lower course of action was to elect to enter such a competition and then whimper about the outcome. One of that year's irregular competitions was for the Cook County courthouse in Chicago. St. Louis's Barnett, Haynes & Barnett won the $5,000 prize, but were passed over in favor of hometowners Holabird & Roche for the job. Some of that prize money may have gone into Barnett, Haynes & Barnett's renegade entry in the St. Louis

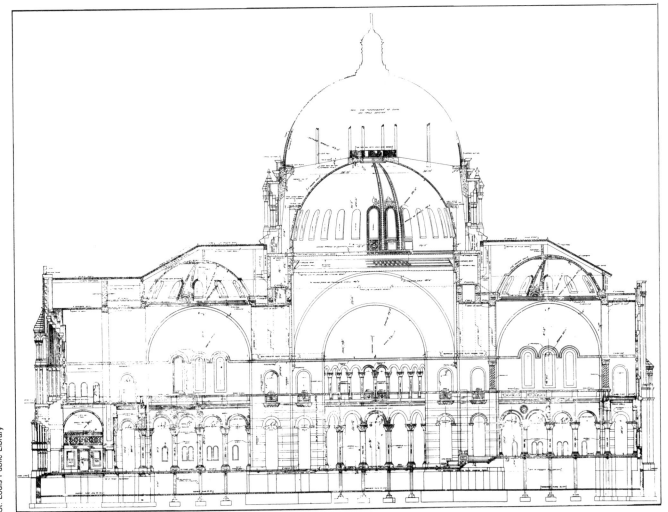

St. Louis "New" Cathedral, longitudinal section, c.1907. Barnett, Haynes & Barnett.

Cathedral sweepstakes.

Dutiful Chapter members must have been dumbfounded to read the following in a 1905 issue of *American Architect:* "We hope that the St. Louis Chapter A.I.A. has not been influenced by the motives assigned to it by the newspapers in voting not to take part in the one million dollar or so Roman Catholic competition. The ostensible reason is that no prizes are offered and that the compensation to be paid the successful architect is wholly inadequate. Behind this is said to be a feeling of irritation because Archbishop Glennon has manifested a distrust of "home talent" by inviting certain French, German and Italian architects to compete. . . . The duty that the profession owes to the public is greater and higher than that which it owes to itself." *American Architect* purred with satisfaction when it announced in March 1906 that a local firm had won.

Chapter conviviality endured in spite of

The Tyrolean Alps restaurant on the Pike was one of the last of the temporary Worlds Fair buildings to be removed. Managed by Tony Faust, Jr., it lingered in affectionate memory thereafter. Widmann, Walsh & Boisselier, 1904.

the one conspicuously recalcitrant but victorious firm. In June, members turned out for a bon-voyage party for Eames, Ittner, and Ernest J. Russell. The trio was bound for the International Congress in London. Russell, a partner in Mauran, Russell & Garden, had just been elected president of the American League of Architects. A friendly report of the send-off in *The Builder* declared St. Louis to be blessed with less friction and more good feeling among its architects than any other big city. Russell's election as Chapter presi-

dent in late 1906 underscored the interlocking bonds between the Club and the Chapter. The bon voyage was also the Chapter's farewell lunch at the Tyrolean Alps, a picturesque Widmann, Walsh & Boisselier leftover from the World's Fair whose continued popularity could not save it from demolition for residential development.

The Exposition Building at Thirteenth and Olive streets, a more venerated landmark, also disappeared from the scene in 1906 as the library board completed ar-

The Western Architect, August 1907

Main Library building competition entry by Barnett, Haynes & Barnett, 1907. The site plan was the reverse of the scheme as adopted— *the library would have been on an expanded block between Locust and St. Charles streets (present Lucas Park), and the park to the south.*

rangements for a Carnegie-endowed library on the site. Partly because of the public nature of the project, the board made heroic attempts to insure a fair competition. However, the initial recommendations from Washington University's Professor Mann, the competition's professional adviser, did not agree with the AIA guidelines.

After objections from Chapter members, the library competition was limited to nine invited firms who were each paid $1,000 to enter—Barnett, Haynes & Barnett; William B. Ittner; Theodore C. Link; Mauran, Russell & Garden (all of St. Louis); Carrère & Hastings; Cass Gilbert; Palmer & Hornbostel; and Albert R. Ross (all from New York). Competitors selected three of their fellows from out of town to sit on the jury; an equal number of local business leaders was appointed by the library board.

During the jury's deliberations, the Chapter entertained the visiting architects at a dinner at the St. Louis Country Club. After the winner was announced on June 6, 1907, competition drawings went on display at the St. Louis Architectural Club, the top five in rank order: Cass Gilbert, William B. Ittner, Carrère & Hastings, Albert R. Ross, Eames & Young. Also-ran Tom P. Barnett, who would later voice his frustrations in *Western Architect,* left for a rejuvenating trip to Europe. Other principals returned to regular practice and duties on national Institute committees.

With Mauran's election at the fortieth annual convention in 1906, St. Louis regained representation on the Institute board of directors. Eames, chairman of the permanent International Congress Committee, was also a member of the

Second Baptist Church in the "Holy Corners" ensemble   *Mauran, Russell & Garden.*
at North Kingshighway and Washington Avenue, 1908.

special committee to test new materials, the Committee on Government Architecture, the Committee for the Preservation of Rock Creek Valley in the District of Columbia, and was, for the second time, Chapter president. Ittner served as chairman of the Committee on State Licensing along with his former partner and the Chapter's former secretary, A. F. Rosenheim—now president of the Southern California Chapter. Young became a member of the nominating committee for Fellows. Mauran found himself on a new committee on the Development of Cities.

Mauran's assignment from the Institute capitalized on his endeavors for the Civic League's St. Louis city plan. Released in January 1907, the plan gained a surge of publicity from a February appearance by the legendary Daniel Burnham at a Civic

League dinner. "It is to be hoped that the interest shown at this dinner was in the plan, rather than in the man," remarked the *St. Louis Builder*. Burnham, who toured the city before his address, urged St. Louisans to tend first to the beautification of the riverfront, a project not included in the $11,200,000 bond issue passed in 1906. That bond issue was due in large part to the Chapter's role in the 1904 *Public Buildings Commission Report*.

In 1908, Chapter members began work on a very different collaborative assignment—the preparation of a model tenement ordinance in cooperation with the Civic League and the Tenement House Association. Not retroactive like recent legislation in notorious New York City, the St. Louis law affected all buildings with two or more families. The legislation was approved without much comment in late March 1909, but enforcement sixty days later brought bitter opposition. Most vocal were members of the Real Estate Exchange, contending that the ordinance would stop growth and deprive the deserving of work.

Both Young, who returned as Chapter president for two years in late 1909, and Russell penned articles supporting the law for the July issue of the *St. Louis Builder*. Russell, a member of the two-year investigative team, described appalling circumstances: people living in basements, hallways without light or ventilation, no access to toilets or bathtubs, among others. "The citizens at large do not realize that anything like such conditions prevail." One of the most public-spirited members in Chapter history, Russell also served on the Public Recreation Committee, a body responsible for ten new playgrounds constructed mostly in congested areas.

Parks, playgrounds, and improved housing conditions were seen by the public as pragmatic precautions in the face of an ever more heterogeneous citizenry. Monumental vistas framed by pretentious governmental buildings were deemed luxuries advocated by an elite that could not even agree on a scheme. Nudged by engineers, landscape architects, and assorted reformers, the Chapter (and the profession) was losing its grip on the reins of the Public Improvement movement.

Although the Civic League's 1907 plan was among those exhibited at the First National City Planning Conference, held in Philadelphia in 1911, the subject had been pigeonholed locally for several years. Nearly all Chapter members professed to be in favor of resuming discussions on civic improvements; the only one who did, William H. Gruen, found himself in a thankless ad hoc conflict with the *St. Louis Republic*. A fire that destroyed the Missouri Capitol on February 5, 1911, finally rallied the Chapter to common cause.

The St. Louis Chapter, like many organizations throughout the state, was visited by a representative from the Capitol Rebuilding Commission before Missouri voters approved a $3,500,000 bond issue on August 1, 1911. Sanguine about progress toward a 1912 competition, the Chapter was startled to learn that Chapter member Louis C. Spiering had withdrawn as professional adviser because of terminal illness. On December 13, the Capitol Commission announced that L. Baylor Pendleton had been selected to replace Spiering. Only one week before, Pendleton had applied for junior membership in the Chapter! An urgent call, including a telegram to Mauran at the Plaza Hotel in New York, went out for a special Chapter meeting as an untested board braced itself for battle.

On December 18, 1911, Secretary George A. Brueggeman sent the first in a series of letters to Jefferson City directing the commission's attention to the Circular (or Code) of Advice on Competitions issued by the Institute. The circular was only part of the latest attempt to slow the profession's lemming procession into competitions; the other part was a monitoring system that combined Chapter and Institute pressure.

When approached formally by the Chapter (and informally by Mauran), Pendleton seemed most agreeable to drafting a program consistent with the code, but the Commission deferred to contrary instructions from the attorney general and issued a program "fundamentally at variance." After review by the subcommittee headed by Young, the offending document was examined by the Institute's Committee on Competitions and its executive committee. With the unanimous disapproval of the competition program by the Institute's network, both the St. Louis and Kansas City chapters passed resolutions in early May 1912 declaring it unprofessional and unethical for any of its members to enter.

Ducking a storm of publicity, Governor Herbert S. Hadley directed the Capitol Building Commission to confer with representatives of the Institute. The Institute assigned four out-of-state notables; Kansas City produced one, and President Ernest C. Klipstein, Young, Mauran, Russell and T. P. Barnett negotiated for the St. Louis Chapter. The matter was settled within days.

All the professional journals carried extensive news of the triumph, the first-ever competition for a state capitol to be held with AIA approval and under its auspices. To assure commissioners that the firm selected could handle the job, the Institute agreed to a preliminary round demonstrating proficiency and experience. From the initial submissions, ten would be selected for the actual competition. The winner would get the work for a six percent fee; the nine losers would each receive $1,000. Three Institute-selected jurors would sit in on each round.

The short list distilled from the preliminary sixty-nine entries included seven firms from New York, one from Philadelphia, with Eckel & Aldrich of St. Joseph and Theodore C. Link & Son of St. Louis completing the field. Professional jurors appointed for the final round—

William B. Ittner, St. Louis; Thomas R. Kimball, Omaha; R. Clipston Sturgis, Boston—and the four-man commission selected Tracy & Swartwout of New York. Each juror was paid $500 plus expenses. Pendleton received $3,000, and the Chapter basked in well-earned congratulations on its moral victory. In 1919 the Institute would direct the Nebraska Chapter to St. Louis for assistance in that state's capitol competition.

But a simple note from Russell to Young in August 1913 precipitated a row rather than a resolution: "Madison County, Illinois has gotten out a Programme for Competition of a new Court House to be located in Edwardsville. Would it not be wise for our Committee to consider it?"

Discovering that the program did not conform, the Chapter's committee on competitions sprang into vigilante action only to discover that Madison County's professional adviser, Professor H. Clifford Ricker, was dean of the Department of Architecture at the University of Illinois, president of the State Board of Architects, and a Fellow of the Institute for thirty-four years. Nonetheless, challenges emanating from St. Louis went first to the Illinois Chapter (Chicago) and then to the Institute's Committee on Competitions.

The AIA code demanded a fee of six percent; Ricker maintained that five percent was acceptable common practice in outstate Illinois. The AIA code required owners to pay extra for any necessary engineering services; Ricker argued that those services were part of the architect's responsibilities. Additional objections to the program included the number and scale of drawings required for the preliminary phase and the adviser's role as

William B. Ittner

Soldan High School, entrance element, 1908. William B. Ittner.

sole judge and jury. At first, Ricker's responses were unyieldingly curt. Eventually, he resigned from the Institute with a salvo of Sherman anti-trust legislation references.

Clearly, the Institute could still not claim consensus among its membership when theory met practice in competitions. Congressmen with constituents who felt wronged by federal competitions had

already forced James Knox Taylor from the Office of Supervising Architect with the repeal of the Tarsney Act in 1912. Colorful testimony from those hearings had been extremely damaging to the Institute, which attempted to refresh its image by creating public information committees in each chapter.

St. Louis responded by awarding its first Chapter medal. In a ceremony held in March 1914 at the University Club, William B. Ittner received a bronze medal with a likeness of Michelangelo for his "marked, meritorious achievement in the design and construction of school buildings." Most of the Chapter's fifty members, including the Institute's new treasurer, John L. Mauran, were present.

In 1915, the Chapter mounted vigorous opposition to the City Plan Commission's monotonous scheme for a Central Traffic Parkway. When the commission was reorganized that September, Louis LaBeaume, a well-born Chapter newcomer, gained a seat. Ernest J. Russell, who had already served two terms in the House of Delegates (predecessor to the Board of Aldermen), became a member after LaBeaume resigned from the commission to accept membership on the board of the City Art Museum. Russell, Chapter president in 1906, was elected again for the 1915-16 terms. A few months later his partner, John L. Mauran, became the second member in Chapter history to be elected to the Institute's highest office.

William S. Eames, who died in March 1915, had ascended to the presidency in a period of optimism and prosperity; Mauran inherited growing discontent within the Institute and an ominous conflict in Europe.

*The Architectural Club announcement for a
preview by Louis LaBeaume of design features of
the Pageant and Masque of St. Louis. The
predecessor of today's Municipal Opera, the
Pageant and Masque was the city's sesquicenten-
nial event. It was staged at the foot of Art Hill
in 1914. In the cast of hundreds, members and
friends of the club played Spaniards of colonial
St. Louis.*

3
Architects and the War: Ready, Willing, and Ignored

A REPORT FROM THE 1915 convention remarked on the uneasy undercurrent of sympathies toward both sides as the first of the expatriate Beaux Arts designers returned home to fight for France. Eastern journals began to warn architects to be careful where they sketched in England or risk being arrested for espionage. By 1916 *American Architect* interspersed bucolic sketches from the front with jarring photos of devastation.

The entire June issue of *Western Architect,* then based in Minneapolis, showcased recent St. Louis work with enviable editorial hyperbole. Special mention was reserved for architect/critic Samuel L. Sherer for his tireless devotion to furthering the art of architecture. Although not a mention of the war could be found, the city and the Chapter were experiencing divided loyalties typical of areas with large German-American populations. Sherer, director of the City Art Museum and honorary member of the Chapter, was among the one-third or more members with ties to Germany. Frederick Widmann was probably the most active member in

fund-raising efforts for the German and Austrian Red Cross; LaBeaume was energetic in organizing the American counterpart.

As 1916 ended with the fiftieth annual convention scheduled for Minneapolis, most Chapter members had reason to anticipate peace in Europe without involvement of the United States. Mauran's address to that convention barely mentioned the war. Delegates found time to avail themselves of excursions into the pine woods to a logging camp and to enjoy the fraternal spirit of LaBeaume's pork-barrel satire, "Washington Pie or the Public Buildings of Medicine Hat." But by the summer of 1917, LaBeaume would be a full-time volunteer with the American Red Cross, Montrose P. McArdle would step into the Chapter presidency, and Mauran would offer the Institute's service to the country, confident that architects' special skills would be appreciated. At Mauran's direction, the new AIA Central Committee on Preparedness distributed a circular to ascertain individual abilities and knowledge among its members. Only one

To the chagrin of architects, their professional services were not in military demand during World War I. However, architecture had homefront uses. It provided noble settings for patriotic activities and displays—in this instance, Isaac S. Taylor's portico of Mercantile Trust, northeast corner of Eighth and Locust. The building was hung with flags and Liberty Loan banners. Partly visible beyond is the Adler & Sullivan St. Nicholas Hotel, where the AIA convention assembled in 1895.

query now seems quaint: "Can you drive a motor car?"

The St. Louis Chapter, among many, passed a resolution and sent telegrams to President Wilson stating that, individually and collectively, the members stood ready for his call to service in any capacity the government might require. The journals, meanwhile, repeated warnings from the British and French not to commit technically trained men to the trenches. (With more than 100 members of the Royal Institute buried in foreign soil, the Architectural Association of London was forced to open a school of architecture for women.)

Ignoring admonitions from the journals, some of their American compatriots became impatient waiting for assignments tailored to training and simply enlisted in the ranks. One of the fortunate, F. Ray Leimkuehler, winner of the St. Louis Architectural Club's student membership prize, left soon after graduation from Washington University in 1917. After ten months at the front in France, Leimkuehler enjoyed four months as an American Expeditionary Force student at the Ecole des Beaux Arts.

As the days dragged on, Institute leaders became increasingly frustrated. Engineers and contractors were at work designing hospitals, barracks, and workers' housing. Repeated attempts to bring architects into the massive building program were rejected outright or ignored.

In St. Louis, a representative of the federal government who arrived to seek candidates for officers to serve as superintendents of hospital and aviation projects sought only the advice of engineers and contractors. Local architects learned of the officer's visit after his departure. Printed efforts to explain this humiliating policy identified a host of possible villains, among them West Point and Annapolis, which offered engineering but not architecture; influential but benighted members of Congress and bureaucrats who classified all architects as elite dreamers, and the Institute itself.

Finally, in September 1917 came the announcement that Maj. Evarts Tracy, former chairman of the AIA Central Committee on Preparedness, had been authorized to form a Camouflage Corps—a new company of architects, painters, and sculptors, but the French rather than the American military actually would perform the "dazzle" work. Instead, Corps members found themselves painting range-finding targets.

Complaining that even their committee on medals and insignia had been overlooked, disgruntled artists and sculptors had the audacity to criticize the design of the Distinguished Service Cross. Only the Red Cross seemed to want something of value from architects—laundered linen drawings that could be transformed into superior bandages.

William Rotch Ware, alpha of *The American Architect,* died in April 1917. In October the journal announced a new team of editors, James Knox Taylor and William H. Crocker. On December 12, the team declared war on the AIA. In retrospect, Mauran and the executive committee's decision not to hold the 1917 convention may have removed the volatile profession's last safety valve. The unpleasant alternative was to conduct the infighting in print. The journal quickly touched off the hostilities by declaring the Institute dormant if not terminal. What followed was unpredictable. Gone were the traditional factions based on age, region, education, political theories.

The first 1918 issue of *American Architect* exploited a long, rebellious letter, "Fetishes and Fallacies," written by the Chapter's past president, Thomas Crane Young, in support of the journal rather than the Institute. "If the war has passed us up as useless, it has also given us leisure which we might improve by looking ourselves squarely in the face and if what we find is not to our liking, we might exercise on ourselves the newly discovered art of camouflage and reappear in another form—perhaps as engineer or contractor-architects."

Young then turned to the "ridiculous Code of Ethics," scriptures set forth for public worship but privately despised by architects. Why should it be a crime to advertise? What other body of sane men would endure public competitions by sanctifying a purification ritual? Why adhere to a fixed percentage fee system? Censured and applauded by other writers, Young, in subsequent correspondence, allowed a future for the Institute only if it undertook broad reform. "It must cease to be, according to all-too-common repute, merely a small circle of self-idolators seated upon imaginary pedestals high above the surging life about them of which they form no part."

All this must have brought great pain to Mauran, who spent more and more time at the Octagon or traveling on official Institute business, away from his private practice and paying railway fares and hotel bills out of his own pocket. His bulletins designed to keep the unhappy membership apprised of its leaders' dogged but discouraging efforts to participate in mobilization only made some of them more churlish, since building at home had virtually ceased.

Materials were either too expensive or subject to restrictions; draftsmen had left for the front or for lucrative jobs in the bloated federal engineering shops. What was left of the construction industry in St. Louis first flung itself into a spate of rehabilitation then cast covetous eyes upon "no end of ramshackle structures" for salvageable materials. The Chamber of Commerce led a movement to give the building commissioner power to demolish all such structures.

Institute members who attended the

fifty-first annual meeting faced a crisis of confidence far more profound than that faced a generation earlier. The Western Association threat primarily had presented an attack from without by those who wanted in. Although reform was also an issue in 1889, talk of reform in 1918 had a strong element of anarchy mixed with bitter disillusionment.

Less than one hundred delegates went to Philadelphia (hometown of the new Chapter president, James P. Jamieson) for the Institute's first meeting in what should have been a building season. President Mauran came right to the point in the opening words of his address: "In these days of stress and patriotic endeavor, when one of the principal activities of a government at war is *building,* why are the architects idle? That is the insistent question on the lips of every member of our profession and of the intelligent citizens who stand amazed in the face of such an anomalous situation."

After announcing his intentions to deal with the "stern reality of things as they are, and not as we would have them," Mauran outlined a chronology of dashed hopes with few accomplishments since the Minneapolis meeting.

He then turned to imputations that the executive committee had failed to inculcate proper appreciation of the profession with official Washington, suggesting instead that the fault lay with "us as individual architects rather than with the professional body of which we are component parts. . . . Have we stood shoulder to shoulder with the budding politician in civic activities . . . or have we held aloof only to be drawn into some City Beautiful movement, born but to die, because we do not insist that our talents are dedicated to the City Practical—and in our professional practice with these officials in their capacity of private citizen and fellow townsman, have we established through efficient and capable professional service rendered, that deep-seated conviction of the administrative ability of an architect, or has the congressional conception of an architect as a dreamer and long-haired creater of useless but expensive dewdaddles come to the Capitol only from the supervising architect's office?"

Finally, Mauran attempted to counter criticisms that the Institute's leadership had made a bad situation with Congress worse by protesting plans and legislation clearly in opposition to the Institute's avowed principles. ". . . if I could believe you counted these battles for the right as errors of judgment in policy, then would I glory indeed in being party to such errors. . . . And so I can say with full conviction: Whatever may be the measure of success in advancing the best interest of our country and our beloved profession, labor toward that end has been given lavishly and without hope of reward other than the satisfaction of having done one's best in a cause to which one's devoted interest has been dedicated."

A motion to amend the Institute's bylaws to allow John Lawrence Mauran to serve a third term failed.

II

Consolidation
1919-1957

by Esley Hamilton

St. Louis Architectural Club at
514 Culver Way

Ladies & Gentlemen who are interested are invited to attend a series of Illustrated Talks on "Early American Architects & Their Work". These talks will be given at the Club House on the First Thursday in each month at 8:30 pm Free of Charge. Please post this Calendar in a conspicuous place. The Dates, Subjects, and Speakers are as follows:

NOV. 3rd 1927   "CHARLES BULFINCH"
   by Professor LAWRENCE HILL
   of the School of Architecture, Washington Univ.

DEC 1st 1927   "THOMAS JEFFERSON"
   by Mr. LOUIS LA BEAUME, F.A.I.A.
   of La Beaume & Klein, Architects

JAN. 5th 1928   "THE PLANNING AND
   EARLY DEVELOPMENT OF
   THE CITY OF WASHINGTON"
   by JOHN LAWRENCE MAURAN, F.A.I.A.
   of Mauran, Russell & Crowell, Architects

FEB. 2nd 1928   "ROBERT MILLS"
   by WILLIAM B. ITTNER, F.A.I.A.
   Architect

MAR. 1st 1928   "Dr. WILLIAM THORNTON"
   by GUY STUDY
   of Study & Farrar, Architects

APR. 5th 1928   "ASHER BENJAMIN"
   by G. F. A. BRUEGGEMAN, F.A.I.A
   Architect

Announcement of a six-month lecture series at the Architectural Club. Many Chapter members belonged to the club, conducted its atelier courses for Washington University, and delivered public lectures such as these. The club's printed announcements characteristically appeared within a plaque frame.

4
Status, Ethics, and Registration

The war is over now!—Your Entertainment Committee is ready to show
some real stuff—The opener is Saturday night January 25th at 8 P.M.
sharp (remember this)—a little
business! and then, The Big Four,
known as the St. Louis Quartet con-
sisting of Messrs. Flesh, Collins,
Niedringhaus and Stark, who have
just returned from France.—They will
entertain you with their latest selections and relate their experiences while
in the front line trenches!—In
addition—a Big lunch and Big
refreshments.

THUS THE ST. LOUIS Architectural
Club announced not just a 1919 social
event, but the beginning of a new era. As
construction rebounded after the austerity
of the war years, architecture correspond-
ingly prospered. This was the heyday of
the period revival, and the many St. Louis
architects skilled in historic styles produced
designs which, though often overlooked today, had real merit. The St. Louis Chapter of the American Institute of Architects
also prospered in those years, although it
seldom could challenge the Architectural
Club in the matter of parties. The
Chapter concerned itself with highminded
questions of professional qualifications,
state registration, and proper rules for

competitions, with an occasional nod at
civic improvement and social
responsibility.

Although the Chapter may have grap-
pled with tedious subjects, it seems to
have done so in comfortable surroundings.
Chapter meetings were dinners paid for by
annual dues. Free dinners at the city's
large hotels, sometimes accompanied by
printed menus, guaranteed good attendance. Meetings of the executive committee were usually luncheons, held almost
exclusively from 1923 through 1931 at the
Benish Cafe, in the basement of the
Chemical Building at Eighth and Olive.

The Chemical Building was ground zero
in any map of Chapter membership. Its

bay windows lighted not only the offices of Mauran, Russell & Crowell, the largest firm in the city, but also those of Hall & Proetz; Helfensteller, Hirsch & Watson; Ernst Janssen; Maritz & Young; Trueblood & Graf; and John C. Stephens. Klipstein & Rathmann were next door at 316 North Eighth, which they remodeled in 1925. The Arcade Building, diagonally across the street, had even more architectural offices, but many of them were not affiliated with the AIA: Tom Barnett, Angelo B. M. Corrubia, Gale Henderson, Jamieson & Spearl, Pleitsch & Price, Oliver Popp, O'Meara & Hills, Study & Farrar, and Thomas C. Young. Other nearby architectural strongholds were the Wainwright Building at Seventh and Chestnut and the Board of Education Building at Ninth and Locust.

The earliest surviving minutes of the St. Louis Chapter of the American Institute of Architects record a meeting of the executive committee held on February 4, 1921. The four men who assembled for lunch on that day all contributed notable examples of the well-made if conservatively designed buildings going up in St. Louis in those years.

Harry G. Clymer (1873-1958) had learned architecture the old-fashioned way, in the offices of Rosenheim and Ittner rather than at a university, and he succeeded to August Beinke's practice after Beinke's death in 1901. On his own, and in partnership from 1908 to 1916 with Francis Drischler, he designed several expensive houses in the private places as well as industrial buildings for Moon Buggy, Polar Wave Ice and Coal, and Ford Motor.

Louis Baylor Pendleton (1874-1963), a native of Atlanta, Georgia, had been practicing in St. Louis since 1900 and was the architect for the division of exhibits at the St. Louis World's Fair. He too had several houses in the private places to his credit, notably in Kingsbury Place, where he later lived himself. Pendleton was to be elected president of the Chapter in 1927 and 1928.

Walter Lincoln Rathmann (1880-1954), president in 1921 and 1922, had been the partner of the older Ernest Klipstein since 1908. They were closely associated with Anheuser-Busch, designing the Bevo Mill on Gravois, the Bevo Plant on Pestalozzi, and the Bauernhof at Grant's Farm. As this meeting was taking place, Rathmann's house was just being started at 6424 Cecil in the newly developing Skinker Heights neighborhood; just a few doors east was the church of St. Michael and St. George, which the firm was to enlarge dramatically later in the decade. In an organization that was known for the cordiality of its members, Rathmann was unusual in being remembered by some of the younger members as an unpleasant person.

Wilbur Tyson Trueblood (1876-1937) had been from 1911 to 1920 the junior partner of Theodore C. Link, whose Union Station and Second Presbyterian Church had associated his name with the Richardsonian Romanesque style in the 1890s. Although Link's firm was one of very few in St. Louis that could claim to have a national practice, Trueblood left it in 1920 to form a partnership with Hugo Graf. He was to serve as president of the Chapter in 1929, succeeding Pendleton.

The secretary of the Chapter, William Wedemeyer (1869-1962), had just resigned from that position. A partner of Albert L. Nelson since 1919, Wedemeyer was largely associated with North St. Louis, where he designed the North Side YMCA, the Sixth Church of Christ, Scientist, and several neighborhood theaters. His son Wesley William Wedemeyer (born 1908) joined the firm in 1932. The elder Wedemeyer's replacement as Chapter secretary in 1921 was W. Oscar Mullgardt (1877-1962). Younger brother of the better-known architect Louis Christian Mullgardt, Oscar Mullgardt joined the St. Louis firm of Shepley, Rutan & Coolidge in the 1890s and remained as it became Mauran, Russell & Garden and then Mauran, Russell & Crowell. He became a partner in the firm in 1930, and president of the Chapter in 1933 and 1934.

Among other items of business that day, Norman Oscar Vegely (1877-1940) was dropped from membership in the Chapter. Vegely had joined the Monsanto Chemical Company in 1917 and after the war became an executive of another chemical firm. He had been on the St. Louis staff of the Philadelphia firm of Cope & Stewardson, winners of the national competition for the design of Washington University.

After the firm was dissolved in 1912 (Cope had been dead since 1902 and Stewardson since 1896), Vegely began his own practice. The few commissions he realized on his own (800 Cella Road in Ladue, 417 Hawthorne and 115 Mason in Webster Park, and 36 Brentmoor in Clayton) suggest that the beautiful Tudor and Georgian detailing of the Cope & Stewardson houses built in fashionable neighborhoods in the preceding decade may have been his work. Nevertheless, Vegely was never able to compete with James P. Jamieson, who had headed the Cope & Stewardson office in St. Louis,

and whose own firm, as successor, continued the association with Washington University and reaped the benefit of the many social contacts thus afforded. Unlamented at the time, Vegely was a real loss to the profession.

Much of the business reported in the few surviving minutes of those years had to do with questions of membership. The Chapter was slow to admit new members, temporizing over each application for months. There were six categories of membership, and shifting from one category to another also required board review. The most prestigious category was Fellow, and St. Louis never had more than a dozen of these at any one time. "Members" belonged to both the national organization ("the Institute") and the St. Louis Chapter, but several men (they were all men) were Chapter Members only. Younger architects could join as Associates, and those just entering the profession could enter as Junior Members for their first few years. Once admitted, members often fell behind in dues, which ranged from five dollars for a Junior Member to twenty-five dollars for a Fellow. In the 1930s as the Great Depression worsened, these seemingly small amounts proved hard to come by, and this necessitated further review. Occasionally the Chapter honored nonarchitects by making them Honorary Associates.

At this distance, the criteria for membership are no longer clear. Certainly, academic credentials were not a determining factor, as Clymer's membership indicates. Nor was practical experience: A. Blair Ridington was told in 1927 that he was not eligible for membership even though he had designed some of the most familiar buildings in the West End, including the chateauesque house at 5215 Lindell and the whole 4400 block of McPherson (the north side from 4417 to 4483). Architects who acted as developers (as Ridington did occasionally) or who were closely associated with particular developers seem to have been at a disadvantage. Hence Gale Henderson, who did dozens of expensive houses in Ladue and the private places, applied for membership in 1922, but his application was held up. The brothers Frank and Thomas Saum, who built houses, flats, and apartments on and near South Grand and in the Central West End, and William P. McMahon, who had a varied career in city and county, are also missing from the membership lists. Nolte & Nauman, who worked extensively with the residential developers George Bergfeld and the Bullock brothers, and Dan Mullen, who worked for Gunther Meier and Norman Comfort on their Ladue and Richmond Heights developments and who designed the Seven Gables Building in Clayton as their office, never were members of the AIA.

The executive board minutes of 1930 reported another question of membership in which the scruples of the Chapter seem to have been working overtime: "This was one of many meetings at which application of George W. Sanger was discussed. Finally decided unanimously to accept application, even tho comment had been made that Sanger might have motive in joining. Only objection raised was the propriety of making application now when his appointment as school board architect is pending."

Sanger, who went on to supervise construction of the New Deal-funded schools in St. Louis, realized the Chapter's reservations by failing to pay his dues, and he

was dropped from membership in 1932. Rockwell M. Milligan, Sanger's predecessor as Commissioner of Buildings for the Board of Education, who had designed Roosevelt and Beaumont High schools and many other schools rivaling the standards William B. Ittner had set before him, had also not been a member of the AIA.

As a result of inconsistent membership policies, the Chapter could not claim in the 1920s to be representative of the profession in St. Louis, not even of the upper stratum. Of eighty-seven firms in a "List of Leading St. Louis Architects" published in 1924, only thirty-five were members of the AIA. Conspicuous among nonmembers were both George D. and Tom P. Barnett, perhaps tainted by their commission to design the Cathedral of St. Louis after a bitterly controversial competition. Tom Barnett, whose name would appear on even the shortest list of notable St. Louis architects, died in 1929; George moved to Los Angeles.

The AIA continued to assert, defend, and protect the professional status of the architect against those who would belittle or inadequately compensate his skills. This had been central to the Institute since its founding in 1857. The Chapter often spoke out against improperly organized architectural competitions, and it also took upon itself (as it continues to do) the role of referee in questions of professional ethics. In the early 1920s, H. Guy Study fell afoul of the Chapter in both these areas. Study (pronounced "Stoody") was one of the most remarkable designers working in St. Louis at the time.

Coming to St. Louis in 1911 after study in France, Study had first joined John J. Roth, who was associated with E. G.

Lewis in the early development of University City. After Roth followed Lewis to Atascadero, California, Study joined Benedict Farrar (pronounced "Fairer"), a socially well-connected St. Louisan descended from the first American physician west of the Mississippi and recognized as an able designer. Study's work was unusual in St. Louis in reflecting an appreciation of the work of Voysey and other Arts and Crafts designers in England.

Study was censured in 1922 for helping to draft a competition in violation of Chapter bylaws for United Hebrew, the oldest Jewish congregation west of the Mississippi, founded in 1841. He pleaded absent-mindedness. The new building on Skinker Boulevard south of Wydown, the temple's fifth home, proved to be one of the largest Jewish temples in the country. It was designed by Maritz & Young, with Professor Gabriel Ferrand of Washington University as consultant. When the congregation moved again in 1990, the temple was remodeled as a library for the Missouri Historical Society.

By this time, Raymond Maritz and W. Ridgely Young, who joined forces in 1921, had come to dominate the market for large period-style residences in the most fashionable neighborhoods. For example, they designed nine of the fifteen houses built on Forsyth Boulevard across from Washington University between 1923 and 1927. Apparently the clients for one of these houses asked Guy Study to take over the project after it had been designed. Late in 1923, John Lawrence Mauran, the patrician head of St. Louis's largest architectural firm, resident of Vandeventer Place and former national president of the AIA, wrote to the

Chapter. He preferred charges against Study for unprofessional conduct, namely copying plans. The following February, Chapter president William A. Hirsch was authorized to send a letter of censure to Study, requiring him to work out an agreement with Young. These professional embarrassments, however, seem not to have done Study any long-term harm. He was named a Fellow in the AIA in 1940.

By the 1920s, several states were setting up registration boards that established professional standards for architectural practice. The AIA encouraged this trend. Missouri, never in a hurry to adopt progressive ideas, was being left behind, as Missouri architects wishing to practice in states that had registration laws had no claim to reciprocity.

The Chapter promoted a registration law in 1924 and went so far as to authorize a special assessment of five dollars per member to finance its introduction, but it became entangled in the similar efforts of the Associated Engineering Societies of St. Louis, and the architects emphatically did not want a blurring of professional distinctions.

The battle to achieve registration went on for so many years that it began to resemble the campaign for women's suffrage. The baton was passed from older to younger generations of the Chapter's successive legislative chairmen as Clymer moved to Michigan and both Klipstein and Trueblood died. P. John Hoener (the first "e" is silent), who had served on the legislation committee as early as 1927, spearheaded the introduction of a new bill in 1938, and Eugene S. Johnson, who had joined the Chapter in 1931, was able to see the bill to passage in 1941.

As constituted under this law, the board

was given jurisdiction over both engineers and architects, but the architects were able to administer their own standards. The board had three architects, three engineers, and a chairman from either profession. Walter Rathmann, nominated by the St. Louis Chapter, was among the first members. Registration number A-1 was issued to the chairman, architect Arthur W. Archer of Kansas City, and the other architect members were 2, 3, and 4. Number A-5 went to William B. Ittner, Jr., and A-6 to Ewald Froese, pronounced "Frayzey," John Hoener's former partner. (The law, Chapter 327 of Missouri Revised Statutes, was rewritten in 1969 to include land surveyors and to add a public member to the board.)

5
The Great Gifts: Steedman and Givens

PROFESSIONAL ARCHITECTS required professional education, and the Chapter worked closely with Washington University, the only architectural school in the state. At the meeting of February 4, 1921, the Professor John Beverley Robinson Scholarship of $50 was renewed for the ensuing academic year. Professor Robinson (1853-1923) had come to Washington University in 1910 after education at Columbia University and a long career as a practicing architect in New York City.

Although dues were raised three dollars per year to cover this scholarship in 1925, by 1930 the Chapter had fallen over $100 in arrears. The cost per semester had risen to $115 by the spring of 1941, and that was the last time the scholarship was awarded until it was revived in 1951 at the instigation of Chapter President Arthur Koelle (pronounced "Kelly").

A second and more important academic fund was established in 1925, when George Fox Steedman (pronounced "Stedman") and Virginia Chase Weddell endowed the James Harrison Steedman Memorial Fellowship in Architecture. It

was named in memory of Mrs. Weddell's first husband and Steedman's older brother, an 1889 graduate of Washington University and, in the words of the deed of gift, "1st Lieutenant U. S. Naval Reserves, Assistant Engineer Officer *U.S.S. Oklahoma* in 1917 and 1918, who at the age of fifty, suffering from a malady curable only by rest, refused to quit his post and knowingly made the great Sacrifice." The Steedmans owned Curtis Manufacturing Company, makers of saws, sawmills, and pneumatic machinery.

George Steedman had a special interest in architecture, both as a bibliophile and a patron; his St. Louis house at 34 Westmoreland was designed by Mauran, Russell & Garden and reflected Edward Garden's interest in the Craftsman movement. His house in Montecito, California, was a Spanish Colonial Revival showplace by George Washington Smith.

The gift establishing the fellowship was $30,000; the anticipated annual income of at least five percent was to constitute the fellowship, which was to be administered by a committee consisting of a representative of the faculty, a representative of the Chapter, and a practicing architect to be selected by the other two and to serve as chairman.

John Lawrence Mauran was the first chairman, chosen by Professor Gabriel Ferrand and Louis LaBeaume. They devised a competition for the fellowship that followed Beaux Arts lines. All applicants had to appear at a set time and place to prepare a preliminary sketch of their solution to the architectural problem put to them that day. They had five to seven weeks to develop this idea into finished form without deviating from it. The prize in the first years was $1,500 for one year of travel and study abroad, "preferably in original research as determined by the committee and under the guidance and control of the School of Architecture of Washington University."

Paul J. Saunders of East St. Louis won the first award. The subject of his problem has been forgotten, but the second problem was a design for an artists' colony. While not all Steedman prize winners remained in St. Louis, many of them did, thereby enriching architectural practice here. George F. Hellmuth, the founder of HOK, for example, won in 1930. Chapter presidents who have been Steedman winners include Kenneth E. Wischmeyer (winner in 1931, president in 1947 and 1948); Lester C. Haeckel (winner 1932, president 1953); Fred Sternberg (winner 1938, president 1959); and Eugene J. Mackey, III (winner 1966, president 1989 and 1990).

In 1974 the terms of the fellowship were altered at the instigation of James Fitzgibbon of Washington University. The competition was made national in scope, and the winner, instead of arranging his own

itinerary in Europe, was sent to the American Academy in Rome for a year. The grateful Chapter made George F. Steedman an honorary member in 1927.

The next year, he and his wife, Carrie, gave his library of about 600 architectural books to the St. Louis Public Library with $50,000 to build a special room for it and another $10,000 for an endowment fund to be administered by the Chapter. The books are said to have been collected by Steedman during a trip to Europe with Louis LaBeaume, Chapter president in 1919 and 1920 and a prominent and outspoken member of St. Louis society. The prize of that excursion was a twenty-three-volume set of Piranesi engravings that had formerly been in the library of the House of Commons.

Another treasure is the 1833 four-volume set of original drawings by A. W. N. Pugin. Steedman had bought it from the estate of Samuel L. Sherer, director of the City Art Museum and occasionally a practicing architect. Steedman encouraged the membership to suggest the names of additional books that could be added to the collection from the endowment.

By 1973, when the *Catalog of the George Fox Steedman Architectural Library* was published, the collection had been more than doubled in size. The room in which it is housed was designed by Oscar Mullgardt of Mauran, Russell & Crowell, with carved paneling and plastered ceiling executed by Victor Berlendis in the Jacobean style suggested by Steedman. Inscribed in the chimneypiece of the working stone fireplace is the dedication, "May students search these shelves for records of honest work and good design and find here inspiration for great achievement."

The room is set into one of the light

*The Steedman Room of the St. Louis Public Library,
designed by Oscar Mullgardt with sculptural details by Victor
Berlendis, a restricted-access treasury off the Fine Arts Room.*

courts of Cass Gilbert's monumental public library and is accessible from the Fine Arts Room, with approval of the fine arts librarian. Chapter members were assured when the room was opened in 1930 that all would recdeive permit cards. Steedman requested the library to seek the advice of the AIA in purchasing books, and the Chapter has appointed trustees to administer this responsibility. In sixty years, only six trustees have served: Louis LaBeaume (died 1961), Kenneth Wischmeyer, Bennett J. Applegate (died 1965), John Albury Bryan (died 1976), W. Philip Cotton, and Richard Bliss.

This long continuity in trusteeship is matched on the librarians' side. Dorothy Breen Neuman, the original librarian, was succeeded by Martha Scharff Hilligoss, who published the catalog and who kept the collection intact when the library wanted to move parts of it to a new rare

book room. She cited the terms of the original gift, by which the trustees and the St. Louis Chapter were authorized to find a new home for the collection if its integrity were threatened. She died in 1987 and was succeeded, after a brief interim under Shannon Paul, by Mary S. Enns Frechette.

That rare book room, constructed in a corner of the main reading room, was removed in later remodeling. The Steedman Collection indeed outgrew its room, and portions were transferred intact to a secured area of the stacks, where their integrity with the collection is maintained. The Chapter made no objection. The library has made a conservation survey of the collection and has completed conservation of the Piranesi volumes at its own expense.

The quiet and withdrawn retired contractor Joseph B. Givens surprised everyone in 1930 by giving Washington University's School of Architecture $800,000. (They were even more surprised a week later when he married for the first time at the age of seventy-one.) Half of his gift was to be reinvested until it reached $1.5 million, when it could be used as a scholarship and general endowment fund. This goal was reached in 1961. The rest was for the immediate construction and maintenance of a building for the school.

The building was completed by 1932 to designs of the campus architects Jamieson & Spearl, with Gabriel Ferrand, head of the school, credited as special consultant. Ferrand had already been responsible, much to the annoyance of Jamieson, for shifting the design of the lower campus near Skinker from Collegiate Gothic to a modernized Adamesque when Bixby Hall

Laying of the cornerstone of Givens Hall, Washington University. The donors, Mr. and Mrs. Joseph Givens, are at left, the Reverend *Karl Morgan Block and Louis LaBeaume at right.*

was built in 1925. His contribution to Givens Hall was the elaborate staircase which occupies the whole center of the building—completed, as it happened, in the depths of the depression.

For years modern architecture remained little more than a subject for debate, because the depression brought an almost total halt to construction in Missouri. In February 1930 Trueblood could still talk about "the great constructive forces in America of today" that "are carrying us on at a tremendous rate." But by 1932

Eugene Klein described a situation of unrelieved bleakness: "Millions of mechanics, in all trades, are idle. Steel plants, lumber mills, brick kilns, stone quarries and hundreds of plants depending on the building industry for their output, are shut down. Consequently, the prices of labor and materials are lower than they have been for a number of years. Buildings of all kinds can be built at bargain prices today, and yet, throughout the nation, the industry lies paralyzed. Idle men, anxious and willing to work, are consuming their small savings, or else being supported by charity."

Architects were among the hardest hit. By the end of 1929 the Chapter made a list of seventeen members who were behind in their dues by a total of $669. Included in the list were past president Pendleton, future president Mullgardt, and Ernst C. Janssen, the only founding member then surviving. Ralph Cole Hall, who with his partner Victor Proetz was doing some of the most interesting work in the city, was further behind than anyone else. By 1932 Hall, Pendleton, and several others had to be suspended. The membership category of Emeritus was created to save Janssen from the same fate.

When Mullgardt became president in 1933, he attempted to keep the membership together by cancelling back dues, reducing dues for 1933, and permitting future dues to be paid quarterly. With many members now paying only $2.50 a quarter, finances still lagged. Someone complained early in 1934 that William B. Ittner was paying his employees only fifty to seventy-five cents an hour, a rate that the executive committee called a "serious threat to the already low standard of living of the employees within the profession."

Even after New Deal programs began to take effect, membership problems continued. Gabriel Ferrand's old partner Austin Fitch was suspended from the Institute in 1937 as was William Wedemeyer's partner, Albert L. Nelson. Raymond Maritz and Ridgely Young, once on top of the profession, were dropped. P. John Hoener lost his chance to be nominated a Fellow because he was not in good standing. By permitting Associates to remain in that category for an additional five years instead of moving up to full membership, the Chapter was able not only to sustain its membership but to grow from eighty-three members in 1930 to 120 in 1938.

6
The Architectural Club

T HE SUDDEN GOOD FORTUNE of the School of Architecture was viewed with a certain wistfulness by supporters of the St. Louis Architectural Club. As John Albury Bryan pointed out in a letter to the editor of the *St. Louis Post-Dispatch* at the time, that institution, which had provided architectural instruction for nearly a decade before Washington University entered the field, had never been blessed by the rich and powerful of St. Louis. Yet it had served many more young men at lower cost; in 1930, tuition was $33 at the club versus $250 at the university. Since 1916 Washington University had held its evening classes at the club, but the club paid the teachers' salaries and all the overhead.

In spite of its financial burdens, the Architectural Club remained very active, as its sprightly party invitations suggest.

Most of the 200-odd members were young, as the *St. Louis Globe-Democrat* reported in 1927. The newspaper also noted that some women were enrolled in the club's classes.

The club offered a free annual lecture series that was substantial in content and popular in appeal. The series for 1927-28, with the theme, "Early American Architects & Their Work," included talks by LaBeaume, Mauran, Ittner, and Study, among others. An annual summer sketch class, meeting every Saturday during the summer ($6 for non-members), offered the Preston J. Bradshaw Prize of $100 for the best collected sketches of the season. Bradshaw (1884-1953) was designing almost as many large buildings as Mauran, Russell Crowell in those years, especially major hotels: the Melbourne, the Coronado, the Chase, and the Forest Park among them.

In 1923, the club was able to purchase the house at 3964 Washington Avenue built in 1888 for the noted photographer Fitz W. Guerin. The clubhouse was the former Guerin stable, built in 1891 behind the house on a private lane that had originally been laid out to give W. W. Culver access to his stable next door. The Guerin stable, designated 514 Culver Way, became the home of the Architectural Club in 1909 and was purchased in 1914. After 1923, the house became the club lounge and a cooperative boarding

John Albury Bryan in the parlor of the Robert Campbell House, 1964. Bryan guided the restoration of the house and grounds.

Past Presidents' Room, Architectural Club, with photo portraits on walls around Cretan stone mantel, gift of Joseph Rasczka.

house with five bedrooms, their occupants employing a housekeeper and a cook.

Over the years, the Architectural Club had many presidents who later held the same post in the AIA Chapter, including Ittner, Brueggeman, Trueblood, Klein, and Mullgardt. In the twenties, the club became popularly associated with John Albury Bryan, described by the *Globe-Democrat* as "young and handsome. Like the rest of the 200 members, he is enthusiastic and ambitious." The native of Chillicothe, Missouri, had himself studied

at the club in 1914 under Guy Study before going on to Columbia University. He served as president of the club in 1924 and 1927, and in the following year published *Missouri's Contribution to American Architecture* under the club's auspices.

The club set up a trust fund to purchase the Guerin house. The fund had seven subscribers, including former club presidents and AIA members Hal H. H. Lynch, F. Ray Leimkuehler and Theron A. Groves, a son of architect Albert Groves. Lynch served as trustee of the fund along with Carl J. Trebus and Herman Frauenfelder. The goal of the trust was to create a fund of $15,000, but this was only accomplished by the loan in 1929 of $13,000 from the Mississippi Valley Trust Company. Daniel J. Carroll, John A. Bryan, and Clarke F. Sanford took over as trustees in 1932. Bryan, one of the residents of the house, became manager in an effort to put the club on a better financial footing.

By 1935 the club had rented the building at 514 Culver Way to the International Institute, a social service agency, but still could not meet its mortgage payments. In 1938 the loan was foreclosed and the property was sold. Bryan's application for membership in the AIA the next year marked the end of an era. Today the old Guerin house is the Reliable Funeral Home, but the old stable is gone. The stone once above its door was found by a cab driver near the house in 1977 and is now installed in the front desk of the AIA Chapter office.

7

Breath of the Modern in the City Beautiful

BRYAN'S BOOK WAS TIMED to show Missouri off to the sixty-first national convention of the American Institute of Architects, which convened in St. Louis Wednesday, May 16, 1928. The Chase Hotel had agreed to host the expected 250 delegates at a room rate of six dollars a day.

Chapter President L. Baylor Pendleton greeted national president Milton B. Medary of Philadelphia and representatives of fifty-eight chapters that morning, and draftsmen and architectural students were invited to lunch. The national directors dined at the Hotel Coronado that evening, and the convention ended Friday with a reception and presentation of awards at the City Art Museum. Speakers at the conference emphasized the importance of city planning and decried the growing tendency to destroy landmarks.

A highlight of the meeting was an exhibition of drawings by Bertram Goodhue, the New York architect who had died four years earlier. Goodhue's late work, especially his public library for Los Angeles and his Nebraska state capitol, had seemed to many architects to point the way toward a new American architecture, and he was eulogized at the convention as a "prophet of logic, high priest of beauty . . . the only true modern." The influence of Goodhue was seen in St. Louis a few years later in the tower of Cardinal Glennon College, designed by Henry P. Hess.

Also on exhibition at the convention were models and drawings of the newly planned Civic Plaza by Hugh Ferriss, a native St. Louisan and nationally known architectural illustrator. The Civic Plaza, with its new courthouse and auditorium, was the most visible result of the great

For the 1928 national convention in St. Louis, Louis LaBeaume wrote and organized a skit disguised as an allegorical pageant. Dressed as the city's namesake, Louis IX of France, he represented the City of St. Louis, and fellow Chapter members played civic roles. This sketch, done by F. Ray Leimkuehler, was printed in The American Architect, *June 5, 1928.*

bond issue of 1923, which had provided architectural opportunities seldom available in St. Louis.

For the most part, the field of public building was closed to architects in private practice. At the federal level, post offices and courthouses were designed by the office of the Supervising Architect of the U.S. Treasury. In St. Louis, schools were designed by the Commissioner of School Buildings, an employee of the Board of Education, and municipal work was the province of the Board of Public Service and its staff architect. The AIA had been pushing since before the turn of the century to open up federal work to local architects, but not until the end of the 1930s did any real change occur in the system

The nationally known delineator of civic visions, Hugh Ferriss, a native of St. Louis, prepared illustrations of Plaza Commission proposals in his evocative style of white-city architecture emergent from shadowy backgrounds. This is the part of the plaza east of Fifteenth Street, looking toward Civil Courts. It and other Ferriss illustrations were published in Southern Architect and Building News, *May 1928.*

established before the Civil War. The Municipal bond issue passed in 1923 was, at $87 million, the biggest that St. Louis or any other American city had ever seen, and it promised work for architects who were not public employees.

Promoted by the slogan, "The Spirit of St. Louis," the twenty-one projects combined City Practical and City Beautiful ideals. One of the most popular projects was the Howard Bend water pumping station on the Missouri River (designed by Study & Farrar), while another diverted the River Des Peres from its meandering channel in Forest Park into an enormous culvert, a nationally-recognized engineering feat. From an architectural point of view, however, the most important project was the Memorial Plaza, which concentrated four projects totaling $21 million in the area adjacent to the City Hall.

This was the first real opportunity the city had had to realize in permanent buildings the Beaux Arts principles of

civic design that had been celebrated at the 1904 World's Fair. Washington, Philadelphia, and Chicago had already started to reshape themselves according to City Beautiful principles, and Cleveland and San Francisco were building new civic centers within their business districts. These were challenging models for St. Louis to emulate.

In the spring of 1925 St. Louis established a Memorial Plaza Commission composed of eight architectural firms and two engineering firms, along with two ex-officio members—the president of the Board of Public Service and Harland Bartholomew, whose title was Engineer of the City Plan Commission. The architects were George D. Barnett, Inc.; the T. P. Barnett Company; Preston J. Bradshaw; Helfensteller, Hirsch & Watson; William B. Ittner, Inc.; Klipstein & Rathmann; LaBeaume & Klein; and Mauran, Russell & Crowell.

The commission set the style and layout

of the buildings cooperatively and then parceled out the detailing. Klipstein & Rathmann are credited with the Civil Courts Building, which was under construction by 1928. Plans for the Municipal Auditorium (later Kiel) were completed by LaBeaume & Klein at the same time, while the Memorial Building, now called the Soldiers' Memorial, was well past the design stage in the offices of Bradshaw and Mauran.

In an article in *Southern Architect and Building News* that spring, Louis LaBeaume described and illustrated a setting of Roman grandeur for the three main buildings. The park blocks on the north side of Market would have terminated in a triumphal arch. A large fountain in front of Kiel would have gone under Fourteenth Street to reappear as a tall jet in front of the Memorial. Another large public building was anticipated in the block between Twelfth and Thirteenth north of Chestnut.

As completed, the Memorial Plaza is considerably less splendid than the Plaza Commission had hoped. Without the lush accessories of the plaza, the relative austerity of the major buildings becomes more apparent. In part, this was budget; the millions in the bond issue proved to be insufficient, and the building projects were rescued only by grants from the New Deal's Public Works Administration.

To a certain extent, however, the look was the choice of the commission. The stripped classical style of the Soldiers' Memorial seemed advanced in 1928. By the time it was finished a decade later, however, it was being compared to work then appearing in fascist Germany and Italy, and it seemed reactionary in contrast to the even greater severity of inter-

national modernism. LaBeaume later wrote, "The architectural revolution that was going forward in Europe hadn't quite reached St. Louis, and the conservative designs for the plaza buildings had been approved. It was too late to change, so there they are for all to see, and for all, including Frank Lloyd Wright, to carp at."

In its dedication booklet, the Soldiers' Memorial claimed to have achieved "a harmonious correlation between Hellenic serenity and the austere simplicity of modern functional architecture," but Frank Lloyd Wright on a visit here called it "a deflowered classic, a Greek thing run through a modernizing mill."

A part of the Plaza, but not within the purview of the Commission, was the new Federal Court House and Custom House at the southeast corner of Twelfth and Market. When the building was announced in 1932, the Chapter, spearheaded by LaBeaume, tried to have its design opened to private architects. The Architectural Club, then headed by F. Ray Leimkuehler, assisted by circulating petitions. As a result, the commission went to Mauran, Russell, Crowell & Mullgardt. Whether this effort ultimately benefitted the public is debatable. When the designs were first published, "An Interested Architect" wrote to the *St. Louis Star* "to voice a vigorous criticism of the wholly inadequate design.

"Experimentation in design perhaps is pardonable with one's own private enterprises, but with a public building, I, for one, cannot feel a designer has the right to deliberately leave the well-beaten paths and take experimental excursions into untrod by-paths, simply because he espies, through the undergrowth, a green patch

Federal Court House and Custom House (also labeled "Post Office" in this drawing) presents the building in the Hugh Ferriss manner as con- *ceived for its Twelfth-and-Market corner by Mauran, Russell, Crowell & Mullgardt. The drawing is signed "J. M. Bennett."*

here and there that seems at a distance alluring. Now is the time to act, and The Star can perform a great public service and keep our city from adding to our galaxy of architectural monstrosities, such as our newly finished Civil Courts Building and our newly finished Police Headquarters Building."

Issues of civic design, which had seemed so remote at the beginning of the period, became more and more contentious as the thirties wore on. Early indications of coming trends appeared in the series of radio talks the Chapter was invited to give in 1930 on radio station KWK and in 1932 on KMOX. Sixteen three-page scripts for these talks survive. Ernest J. Russell wrote

two of them, and Trueblood, LaBeaume, Angelo B. M. Corrubia, Klein, and Hoener contributed others. Professor Lawrence Hill of Washington University gave the same talk twice, but he was so enthusiastic about the possibilities of radio that he proposed a lengthy series, to be delivered by himself, outlining the whole history of architecture. Most of the talks emphasized the familiar themes of the AIA: that the architect is a professional and that his service is not an extravagance but an economy.

Lawrence Hill was remembered by Charles Eames as one of the greatest teachers he ever had. In his talk, "The Trend Toward Modernism in Architecture,'' Hill characterized the period architecture of the early twentieth century as ''coquetting with past forms, adapting them, to be sure, with great ingenuity to modern uses, but always invoking the query, 'Is this really the language of our scientific age? Are we eternally doomed to the repetition of classic columns and Gothic tracery?''' He defined Modernism as ''conscious awakening to the significance of our epoch with the resolution to deliver its art from the thralldom of the past.'' He saw Modernism as a wide cultural movement to which architecture, ''too costly to yield itself lightly to the reckless experimenting of the other arts,'' was nevertheless slowly being drawn.

Eames, born in St. Louis, was graduated from Washington University and then taught there while practicing locally in a small way. He recalled that to him Modernism meant Frank Lloyd Wright and Eliel Saarinen, since the Bauhaus was little known. His interest in Wright led to his being asked to leave the Architecture School. ''I didn't worry about it as incompatible with the Beaux Arts school because Wright knew architecture,'' Eames later remembered. ''It was just a little bit mysterious to me why, even though it was a Beaux Arts school, they couldn't embrace people like Wright. Ferrand was absolutely rabid on the subject.

''Actually Ferrand, in later years, began to be taken by the modern school; in one of the few great architectural debates in St. Louis, Gabriel Ferrand undertook to defend the issue of the modern international style. And the poetic justice came when Louis LaBeaume, taking the classic side, actually cut Ferrand to ribbons

because Ferrand demonstrated that, while he was a Beaux Arts architect, he knew neither the modern nor the classic side of the argument. I think it just about killed Ferrand.''

The Chapter began to be reinvigorated in the late thirties by some of the pioneers of the new architecture. Charles Eames went to teach at Cranbrook, but Harris Armstrong became an associate member in 1936, Charles Nagel and Frederick Dunn joined in 1937, and Joseph D. Murphy transferred his membership from Kansas City. Kenneth E. Wischmeyer, the former Steedman winner and son of another Chapter member, joined in 1940.

Armstrong's medical office for Leo Shanley, built in Clayton in 1935, was the first International Style building in the midwest—scorned by his old teachers at Washington University until it won the silver medal at the Paris World's Fair of 1937. Armstrong had the good fortune to attract a large number of physicians, one of the few groups financially able to build in those years and, in contrast to most architectural patrons of the previous decade, open by training and temperament to innovation.

Nagel, son of a prominent St. Louis attorney, and Dunn, a Montanan whom Nagel had met at Yale, won attention for their design of St. Mark's Episcopal Church in St. Louis Hills. It is filled with references to the Baroque, but at the time it was seen as ''a new and bold departure from the traditional'' and hailed for the way it integrated the arts, with sculpture by Sheila Burlingame and stained glass by Emil Frei. Joseph Murphy came to teach at Washington University and eventually became dean of the architecture school. He teamed up with Wischmeyer in 1938

The Shanley Building by Harris Armstrong, Maryland at Bemiston, 1935.

in the competition for the Municipal Opera Arcade in Forest Park. Their airy winning design, ornamented by sculptural reliefs in the rounded pediments, is overlooked by most theatergoers hurrying to their seats, but it was much admired in its day.

William Bernoudy returned in 1936 from four and a half years with the Taliesin Fellowship, the school run by Frank Lloyd Wright at his homes in Wisconsin and Arizona. The house that Bernoudy built in 1939 with Edouard Mutrux for Mutrux's sister, Suzette Talbott, introduced the Wrightian ideal to St. Louis. Neither Bernoudy nor Mutrux joined the AIA, however, until 1959.

8
The Riverfront and the New Deal

On December 11, 1933, the Chapter recommended Wilbur Trueblood as district officer for the new Historic American Buildings Survey. This was remarkably quick work, since the initial proposal for HABS, as it came to be known, had been written in a Georgetown apartment on a Sunday afternoon only a month before. That so prominent an architect would be willing to take on such a project, which paid ninety cents to a dollar ten an hour for a thirty-hour week, was another indication of the dire economic conditions of the time.

The Historic American Buildings Survey was created by architect Charles E. Peterson to record important examples of America's architectural heritage in photographs and measured drawings. The National Park Service, initiator of the project, arranged with the AIA to assure professional standards and with the Library of Congress to be the repository and reference source for the completed work.

Locally, a committee was set up to select buildings to be recorded. It included the presidents of the St. Louis and Kansas

City chapters, one other architect (initially LaBeaume's partner Eugene Klein) and two laymen. Trueblood hired more than thirty architects, and by April 1934 was able to mount an exhibition at the Public Library of the work accomplished. To mark the occasion, McCune Gill, an attorney and title insurance executive who was also an enthusiastic amateur historian, gave a talk on the history of Missouri as reflected in its buildings.

Trueblood died unexpectedly on May 23, 1937, but by the beginning of 1938, the Library of Congress had accepted HABS records of 140 Missouri buildings. Virtually all of them dated from before the Civil War. Of these, most were recorded by one or two photos only. Thirteen properties had been recorded by measured drawings, three in Ste. Genevieve, two in Kansas City and eight in St. Louis.

This somewhat subjective honor roll turned out to be a forecast of historic preservation battles to come. The Eugene Field House at 634 South Broadway (HABS M0-31-3) was threatened with demolition at the very time it was being

"Preliminary Study for a National Memorial to Thomas Jefferson and the Louisiana Purchase on the Mississippi River—St. Louis, Mo. by The St. Louis Chapter AIA." This rigidly formal conception, published December 28, 1933, was drawn by W. O. Mullgardt, then Chapter president, from data gathered by the City Plan Commission and McCune Gill. Lines of pavilions extend north and south of a stocky tower with a Jefferson statue on the Old Courthouse axis. This axis is further defined by flanking colonnades and fountain basins—one of the squares became Luther Ely Smith Park. Other landscaped strips and sunken courts are symmetrically positioned between trafficways. Clusters of Art Deco-ish office buildings include one on the site of the deleted Old Cathedral.

recorded, but a group of private citizens was able to save it. It was opened to the public at the end of 1936, the first such historic shrine in the area.

Other preservation successes to come included HABS M0-12, the Robert Campbell House; M0-14, the Chatillon-DeMenil House; M0-16, the Captain Lewis Bissell Mansion; and M0-31-8, the Old Courthouse (the most extensive project, with seventeen sheets of drawings). But more than half the buildings would be lost, including M0-31-2, the Grant-Dent House at Fourth and Cerre, where Julia Dent married Ulysses S. Grant; and M0-31-5, the Old Rock House on the riverfront. The biggest challenge (and biggest loss) was the St. Louis riverfront itself, which had

Luther Ely Smith, a 1941 photograph.

long since become a backwater of the business district. Trueblood photographed four old buildings on North Main (First Street) and two others nearby. The riverfront in those years still had most of the warehouses and commercial buildings that had been built after the disastrous fire of 1849 in the "fireproof" construction of that era, cast iron. The architectural historian Siegfried Giedion was one of the first to draw national attention to the historic value of this district in his book, *Space, Time and Architecture,* but that was in 1941. In the 1930s, people such as Trueblood and John Albury Bryan who could see this were in a tiny minority.

Most people in 1933 saw the riverfront as a collection of fast-deteriorating buildings. Once they were cleared away, though, the site had great potential for monumental civic treatment in the City Beautiful vein. A week after Trueblood had been recommended to HABS, the Chapter's executive committee met to discuss a new proposal for improving the riverfront. From the minutes: "A letter from Mr. McCune Gill to the Mayor, which was passed around for everyone to read, proposed a memorial on this open space. Mr. Bartholomew enlarged on this idea by suggesting a great memorial to Thomas Jefferson, recognizing in the memorial the states of the Louisiana Purchase and of the Northwest Territory.

"The General Council on Civic Needs requested drawings showing such a scheme, and asked architects to do the work. The Executive Committee approved of the idea of helping to do this. Proposal that the drawings be made at the University and that draftsmen be employed at the Chapter's expense was approved." By New Year's a drawing was ready, and the

draftsman Mr. [Bernard] McMahon [later a prominent architect and developer] was paid $50.

For the Chapter to permit drawings to be made gratis was a major concession of policy, evidence of someone's persuasiveness. By contrast, Clinton Whittemore had been turned down in 1924 when he asked for drawings to promote fund-raising for the Bishop Tuttle Memorial at Christ Church Cathedral, which was intended to be a major downtown community center.

The Council on Civic Needs mentioned in these minutes was headed by attorney Luther Ely Smith. It was he who approached Mayor Bernard Dickmann with the original concept for the riverfront. He became chairman of the Jefferson National Expansion Memorial Association early in 1934, and it was his energy and determination more than anyone else's that kept the vision alive through one setback after another. The park between the Old Courthouse and the Arch is named for him. Although Smith was never honored by the AIA, he is remembered by Robert Elkington as a friend of architects; a visit to his home at 5321 Waterman Avenue after work was always good for a drink.

At first, the riverfront project moved forward with a speed typical of the New Deal. President Franklin D. Roosevelt authorized a federal commission in June 1934 and its first meeting was December 19 at the Jefferson Hotel. There, Louis LaBeaume proposed a group of buildings on axis with the Old Courthouse with murals, obelisks, and a great dome. LaBeaume lived across the street from Smith, and his design, though effective in suggesting the possible grandeur of the project, produced such criticism by some architects that LaBeaume almost resigned from the Chapter. But that was behind the scenes.

In public, progress continued in 1935, when President Roosevelt designated the downtown St. Louis riverfront as part of the National Park system. This had the benefit to the AIA of creating a permanent National Park Service staff. John Albury Bryan joined it as research historian and remained for twenty-three years. Charles E. Peterson, the man who originally proposed HABS, moved to St. Louis from Washington and soon became involved in Chapter affairs. These two men reinvigorated the Chapter's interest in historic preservation at a time when the city could tear the cupolas and finials off the roof of City Hall with little objection from anyone except Guy Study.

The Works Progress Administration (WPA) has become the most famous of the New Deal agencies that provided work relief to the nation's unemployed, but the primary benefits for architects came from the Public Works Administration (PWA). The PWA made construction grants to states, municipalities, school districts, and other units of government. In many Missouri counties, no construction of any kind took place in those years except with PWA support. PWA projects in St. Louis were still monopolized by staff architects of the sponsoring agencies, but elsewhere private firms had unrivaled opportunities.

Firms such as William B. Ittner that already had experience with public buildings were favored. Marcel Boulicault, who had made a reputation designing finely crafted Period style houses in the twenties, prospered by turning to state hospitals, prisons, and government office buildings. Eugene S. Johnson and Albert

C. Maack designed two of the nineteen new courthouses that the PWA funded around the state.

New Deal planners anticipated that private organizations would be willing to sponsor low-rent housing with federal support. In the first round of funding, however, only twelve such groups qualified in the whole country. One was in St. Louis—the Neighborhood Association, which operated a settlement house on the near North Side. Its director, J. A. Wolf, had visited Berlin and Vienna to study their celebrated housing projects, and he had been working with P. John Hoener and Ewald Froese (of Hoener, Baum & Froese) on a similar housing project to be built at Seventh and Biddle in the heart of the city's worst slum area.

It became Neighborhood Gardens, which from a social point of view remains the city's most successful low-rent housing project. It provided a model for the low-rise, separate-entrance designs of the city's first two *public* housing projects, both built in 1941. Carr Square Village on the north side was designed by Klipstein & Rathmann for Negroes, while Clinton-Peabody Terrace on the south, by Mauran, Russell, Crowell & Mullgardt, was for Caucasians. Hoener remained for many years the force behind the Chapter's interest in housing and related planning issues.

Ernest J. Russell was even more closely associated with planning. Born in London in 1870, he came to St. Louis in 1898. He became the first chairman of the City Plan Commission in 1917. On his retirement from that position in 1937, the *St. Louis Globe-Democrat* wrote, "In measure not to be duplicated in any other individual, Ernest J. Russell has given delightful

*P. John
Hoener*

Neighborhood Gardens, private low-rent housing with federal support. Hoener, Baum & Froese, 1935.

welding to utility and beauty in city planning for St. Louis, of which he has been leader and spokesman for the last twenty years.''

Russell served from 1932 to 1935 as national president of the AIA, a position his partner Mauran had held from 1916 to 1918. In 1933 the Chapter held a special meeting to honor him. He served again as chairman of the Plan Commission in 1944 and remained a member until 1949. By then he was recognized as the dean of architects in St. Louis. Russell lived in the house at Cabanne and Goodfellow that had been designed in 1886 by H. H. Richardson for Henry S. Potter—considered by many one of the architectural treasures of St. Louis. Russell bequeathed it to the city on his death in 1956, and the city tore it down for a playground.

By 1941 St. Louis architects were beginning to be caught up in America's preparations for war. Benedict Farrar went to Washington that February to design buildings for the War Department. He was joined in September by William

B. Ittner, Jr., leaving the Chapter without a president. The secretary of the Chapter, Charles E. Peterson, then announced that he had been classified 1-A by the Selective Service System. Treasurer Fred Hammond, a World War I pilot, was in the U.S. Naval Reserve and was subject to recall at any time. The Institute urged each chapter to appoint a committee on civil defense ''to make the architectural profession a force in this type of program.'' Eugene Klein chaired the local committee.

After Pearl Harbor, the only person left on the executive committee who could sign checks for the Chapter was vice-president Lawrence Hill; since they required two signatures, the checks had to be mailed to Hammond, by then working in Washington. Oma Koch had to be recruited, at a cost to the Chapter of $60, to prepare the treasurer's report for the year. She was the treasurer of the Britt Printing and Publishing Company, which handled the Chapter's mailings.

The 1944 membership list reported thirteen members in the armed forces. F. Ray Leimkuehler became Maj. Francis R. Leimkuehler, the highest military rank in the Chapter. He had gone to Washington in 1940 with HABS, then joined Farrar, Ittner, and Hammond on the team that designed and supervised the construction of the Pentagon Building. After his commission, he spent three years in England in the U.S. Army Corps of Engineers. At the other end of the scale, George F. Fritzinger was a private at nearby Scott Field in Illinois.

A surprising number of these midwesterners were in the Navy, including Peterson, who served as a civil engineer on the staff of Admiral Chester A. Nimitz. Frederick Dunn, Leonard Haeger, and Kenneth Wischmeyer were also in the navy. Lt. Robert L. Fischer was on the *U.S.S. Warren,* an attack transport in the South Pacific, while Lt. G. Vietor Davis was on the *U.S.S. Gauger* in the Caribbean and the Mediterranean. Thus did the war serve to level the classes: Davis was the son of J. Lionberger Davis of Brentmoor Park, a wealthy civic leader and art collector, and after the war his friend Laurence Rockefeller came to his wedding to Maude Scudder Overall, a great-granddaughter of Samuel Cupples, another civic titan.

For another group of young architects, the war had other implications. American citizens of Japanese ancestry who were living on the western states were being forced into internment camps. Several of them came to Washington University, where they were not considered threats to national security. Richard Henmi, Ichiro Mori, Gyo Obata, and Fred Toguchi became student associates of the Chapter,

but there were others, including George Matsumoto, Henmi's friend Ted Ono, and Obata's friend Kyoshi Mano.

Henmi's experience was perhaps typical. He was attending the state college in his home town of Fresno when the war came. He was sent with his family in May 1942 to the "Fresno Assembly Center," actually the fairgrounds, until he could be admitted to an inland school. Accepted by the University of Colorado, he arrived at Boulder late in August to find a Navy training center there, so he had to find another school whose fall semester started later. Washington University welcomed him, largely, Henmi remembers, because of the efforts of Arno Hauck, director of the campus YMCA. Later Henmi's family was able to move to St. Louis under the sponsorship of Mrs. Thomas Sayman.

These men, thrown together by the fortunes of war, scattered after their graduations, but many remained friends. Matsumoto went to North Carolina State, Mano and Obata to Detroit, Toguchi to Cleveland. Henmi and Toguchi married sisters. Ichiro Mori, labeled a potential enemy during the war, became a supervising architect for the U.S. State Department and traveled around the world designing United States embassies; his last project was in Tokyo.

Eugene S. Klein, although not in uniform, became a casualty of the war. He was appointed architect for the Seventh Construction Quartermaster's Zone in 1941. On November 4, 1944, while driving to inspect some army work at Fort Leonard Wood, he suffered a severe head injury in an automobile accident, and he died of its effects a little over a year later.

9
New Technology, Public Housing, and the Gateway Arch

At a meeting in 1944, Oliver L. Parks, the founder of Parks College of Aeronautical Technology in nearby Cahokia (now Parks College of Saint Louis University), spoke on aviation and offered to teach any six members of the Chapter to fly in six hours. Nobody took him up on his offer. Of six topics proposed for a joint meeting with the engineers in 1945, three were about television. A few years later, Arthur Holly Compton, Nobel laureate and chancellor of Washington University, spoke on "The Relationship of Atomic Energy to Architecture and Regional Planning." Discussions of emerging technologies were beginning to dominate Chapter meetings.

Robert Elkington recalled that when he joined the Chapter, "W.W. II had just ended. The architectural profession was trying to get back on its feet. 'Contemporary' architecture was coming in. Most travel was by train or automobile. Air-conditioning was just being developed. Architects had time to argue their philosophy of design, and kindred souls gathered to talk."

Still, as the Chapter grew, many of its concerns remained the same as in earlier decades. Questions of membership, professional ethics (especially advertising), and support for Washington University remained constants. The Chapter sought cooperation with related organizations, including the Missouri Society of Professional Engineers, the Producers Council (a national organization of manufacturers of building materials and equipment), and the Associated General Contractors, representing the construction industry.

Almost every year at least one large project, such as a conference or a competition, was planned to promote architecture. And with the increased emphasis on social responsibility so characteristic of the postwar era, the Chapter took a more active role in civic issues.

Following the war, the Institute looked forward to reaching a membership of 5,000. "Perhaps within a few years," wrote C. Julian Oberwarth, membership secretary, "we may even boast a membership of fifty-one percent of all the architects and become the true voice of the

Ernest J. Russell and Arthur Holly Compton, prior to Compton's address to the Chapter April 3, 1951.

profession." But, he continued, "we should have no goal, but strive incessantly for the kind of perfection in membership which will afford us the opportunity to make our profession the real force in the American social order which we know it should be." Exactly what "perfection in membership" meant was not defined, but "the cutting of fees and the execution of work for the real estate trade catering to their standards"—charges leveled against one unsuccessful applicant for membership in the St. Louis Chapter—were certainly not permitted.

The AIA's standards of behavior applied to all. When Frank Lloyd Wright was proposed for the 1949 Gold Medal, objections were raised to his personal morals and his unethical conduct in underbidding and stealing jobs. The Baltimore chapter went on record as opposing the honor. St. Louis supported it, but only by a vote of twelve to eight.

Advertising of any kind was strictly forbidden, and occasionally architects would run afoul of this rule through efforts to support clubs, neighborhood groups, and other civic interests. Guy Study was

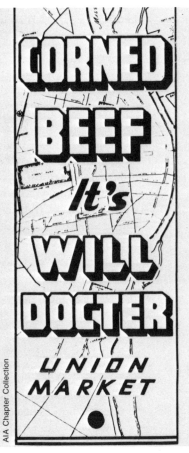

STUDY, FARRAR & MAJERS

Architects

GArfield 2189

Churches, Schools, Commercial Buildings

Architects of

St. Luke's Roman Catholic Church

Our Lady of Lourdes Church

St. Peter's Episcopal Church, Ladue

Emmanuel Episcopal Church, Webster Groves

Mary Institute

Gymnasium at Parks Air College

Alton Brick Co.

3832 W. PINE   **JE. 6677**

Manufacturers and Distributors

Structural Clay Products

Concrete Products

Glazed Tile — Glass Block

A forbidden advertisement for an architectural firm, printed in The Gridiron Magazine, *November 25, 1948. It brought a reprimand to Guy Study.*

severely chastised for running an ad for Study, Farrar & Majers in *The Gridiron Magazine,* where it appeared on the same page as Town Hall Restaurant, Blue Ridge Bottling Company, and Will Docter's corned beef.

Other malefactors were Ernest Friton, reported advertising in the Lions Club paper, and Henry Hess, seen in the *St. Louis Register,* the archdiocesan journal. Bernard McMahon ran an ad for a special lavatory unit he had designed, using the initials AIA behind his name when he wasn't even a member. In spite of this lapse, however, he was admitted to membership the following year.

The Chapter remained close to Washington University. Lawrence Hill, the head of the Architecture School from Gabriel Ferrand's death until 1948, was an active member of the Chapter, as was his successor, Joseph D. Murphy, the first to hold the title of dean. The Chapter established a special membership category of Student Associate in 1940. Among the first admitted were Richard Bliss, who won the Steedman prize in 1942, and Susan Sallee, later Mrs. Charles Lorenz, the first woman to be admitted to the Chapter and, in 1947, probably the first to be registered by the State of Missouri.

After the Student Associate category was eliminated about 1953, a student chapter was set up at the Washington University, with its own letterhead. The student chapter produced a small guide to the architecture of St. Louis in 1955, the first publication of its kind. Charles Hansen was elected student chapter president that year, while Ted Christner was student body president. As the enthusiastic charter members graduated, however, the campus chapter disappeared.

The AIA Chapter awarded scholarships whenever funds were available. In 1956, for instance, the Chapter served as intermediary for one of six scholarships given nationally by the National Board of Fire Underwriters, and Thomas H. Teasdale of Clayton received $800. The Chapter also gave an annual award to the graduating student with the best academic record. This was called the AIA Medal, although a book was given as the prize. Rex Becker won it in 1935, Harry Richman in 1949. The presentation to Richman of *Mont-Saint-Michel and Chartres,* by Henry Adams, was at the annual summer party at St. Albans.

The summer parties of those years are better remembered than many of the accomplishments in which the Chapter may have taken greater pride at the time. Held as the June meeting, these events lasted from early afternoon into the evening. Frequently they were at the Barn Inn in St. Albans, overlooking the Missouri River in Franklin County. Other sylvan retreats included Grant's Farm, the

August Busch estate; Vouziers, the Joseph Desloge estate; and Fercrest, the cast-iron home of Francis Mesker, with its funicular descending to the Missouri River. Harris Armstrong's champagne punch was considered a necessity at these parties, so much so that it was sometimes specified in the executive committee minutes.

In addition to general and executive meetings, many members were on call for meetings of committees. The Chapter appointed as many as seventeen committees each year, and frequently it was these small working groups that tackled the hard issues. Not all the committees were overburdened, however, as the following annual report attests:

> Report of Committee on Civic Design
> January 28, 1947
> Your committee had one meeting during the year and without having had a specific task assigned to it by the officers, did not bestir itself into activity on its own account. Such is the frailty of human behavior. The committee is glad to report there were not to the committee's knowledge any unfortunate developments during the year against which its voice might have been added in perhaps futile protest. At our one meeting it was most difficult to keep the attention of the members on the work in hand because of the range of ideas affecting the profession with which their minds were bristling. All perennial subjects brought up at Chapter meetings were discussed pro and con and with as good results.
> The committee on Civic Design is glad to report that it is in favor of its subject matter, civic design.
> Fred R. Hammond, Chairman

As Hammond implied, the Chapter's protests were often futile. The Chapter

Recipe for the traditional punch, recorded in Chapter minutes and published in WAL St. Louis Cook Book, *St. Louis Chapter AIA, 1981.*

spoke out loudly and bitterly, for example, when Vandeventer Place was proposed as the site of a Veterans Hospital early in 1947. John Albury Bryan, the long-time chairman of the Committee on Preservation of Historic Sites and Buildings, expressed dismay that the newspapers didn't seem to care whether this street, which many thought the most magnificent of the city's private places, remained intact or not. He accused the city government of having precipitated the collapse of the place by levying outrageously high special assessments for the unnecessary widening of Enright Avenue bordering it. "Too many crimes are committed in the name of Progress!" he concluded.

The loss of Vandeventer Place was part of the broader trend toward clearance as a solution to urban problems. The city reshaped itself through expressways and urban renewal. Public housing became a major feature of the inner city in part because it was another rationale for slum clearance. The carefully reasoned low-rise housing projects pioneered by P. John Hoener began to be challenged by the more dramatic high-rise visions of Le Corbusier.

This issue came to a head in the design of the John J. Cochran Apartments, the public housing complex planned for the tract from Seventh to Ninth just west of Neighborhood Gardens. There, the low-rise plans of Jamieson, Spearl, Hammond & Grolock, produced at a cost of $70,000, were abandoned, and new high-rises were commissioned from George Hellmuth.

Chapter president Arthur E. Koelle sent a letter to Mayor Joseph M. Darst, criticizing this decision: "If the Housing Authority considers it necessary to abandon the government approved plans, we believe that they should construct buildings affording greatest comfort and safety for their occupants rather than ones which under actual use may prove to be only monumental Public Buildings, monuments to the vanity of Public Officials."

Mayor Darst's background was in real estate, and he had strong opinions on this subject. He told reporters, "I believe we will get housing more attractively constructed and more economically built with new plans than with the old ones. Look at the project on Chouteau Avenue [Clinton-Peabody Terrace]. We tore down slums and recreated slums."

This criticism must have stung Koelle, who had been associated with Klipstein & Rathmann when the firm had designed Carr Square and was a partner in the successor firm of Rathmann, Koelle & Carroll. In a second letter, he questioned "the advisability of housing families in the low income bracket in six and thirteen story apartments, as suggested by the architect for the proposed project. Criticism has been made by the Administration of the two completed housing projects [Clinton-Peabody and Carr Square] but this Committee fails to see in the sketches as recently presented in the press qualities of design other than height, which would make them superior to what has been done."

Hellmuth, son and nephew of prominent turn-of-the-century St. Louis architects, had been working in Detroit with Smith, Hinchman & Grylls since the beginning of the war, and this raised another issue. Koelle regretted that the Housing Authority "did not deem it advisable to consult with established taxpaying architects, rather than employ one who had been practicing in Detroit." Darst pointed out that Hellmuth planned to move back, and indeed the firm of Hellmuth, Yamasaki & Leinweber opened offices in St. Louis that June. Here they acquired a near monopoly on the design of public housing, following Cochran with the Joseph M. Darst Apartments at Twelfth and Chouteau and the Wendell 0. Pruitt Homes (later notorious as Pruitt-Igoe) at Jefferson and Cass.

The post-war baby boom created a bonanza for architects in the design of schools. The St. Louis Board of Education sought voter approval for a $17 million bond issue in 1951 and asked the Chapter for its support. Hellmuth was appointed to the Citizens Advisory Committee, while William B. Ittner, Jr., Charles Lorenz, and Kenneth Wischmeyer were asked to review the proposed building program in conjunction with representatives of the Associated General Contractors.

The School Building Committee found that the proposed budget, while large, was inadequate to the work at hand and would result in cramped sites, small buildings, and inequitable distribution of facilities throughout the city. F. Ray Leimkuehler,

since 1948 the supervising architect for the school board, took personal offense at this criticism. "I take a poor view of the whole idea of submitting my work for judgment by my peers. It might be implied that there is some question with regard to my competence." But after the bond issue was passed, funds did prove insufficient, and much of the plan had to be dropped.

The Chapter continued to take an active interest in the development of the Jefferson National Expansion Memorial after the war. During the war and for several years thereafter, the site served as a 4,500-car parking lot, and there were those in the business community who favored keeping it that way. Luther Ely Smith and the Jefferson National Expansion Memorial Association raised money to hold a national design competition and hired Philadelphia architect George Howe to organize it. Smith and Howe explained their concept of a two-tier competition to the Chapter early in 1947, and after the initial deadline that September 1, they returned with the jurors and other members of the association.

The panel of seven jurors included architects Richard Neutra and William Wurster, both of whom would later win the AIA Gold Medal, as well as St. Louisans Louis LaBeaume and Charles Nagel, the latter by then director of the Brooklyn Museum. The initial phase of the competition drew 172 entries. These were reduced to five, and the designers were given five more months to produce a finished proposal. Harris Armstrong, who had produced a riverfront design in 1944 for *Architectural Forum,* was the only St. Louis architect in the final five, and the only finalist working alone.

The winners were announced February

Judges of the Jefferson National Expansion Memorial Competition, on steps of the Old Courthouse. From left: Herbert Hare, Roland A. Wank, Charles Nagel, Jr., Louis LaBeaume, Fiske Kimball, Richard J. Neutra, George Howe, and William W. Wurster.

18, 1948. Eero Saarinen's winning design, a steel arch rising from an urban forest, was by far the most ambitious of the five and presented the most problems in realization. The Chapter expressed the hope "that means will be found to carry out the design in all the grandeur of the original conception." In the meantime, the competition brought the city much favorable publicity, including an entire issue of *Progressive Architecture.*

Conferences and conventions loomed large on the Chapter's agenda in those years. The national convention and the Central States Regional Conference were annual events, and conferences about special concerns became more frequent. Gone were the days when it would occur to a Chapter member to suggest that attendance at the national convention be restricted to keep it from becoming too large.

The Institute's Committee on Urban Planning and Housing hosted a conference on "The Architect and Public Housing" at the Hotel Jefferson in 1950 for reflections on the Public Housing Act, passed in the previous year. Harland Bartholomew, one of the foremost urban planners in the nation and long an honorary associate of the Chapter, was one of the speakers. Kenneth E. Wischmeyer, another participant, was second vice-president of the Institute at the time.

Two years later, for a conference on church architecture, the Chapter and the Bureau of Church Architecture of the National Council of Churches were cosponsors, with the participation of the Metropolitan Church Federation of Greater St. Louis. One drawback to holding national meetings in St. Louis was alluded to by the head of the Bureau when he wrote that he had "cleared with the Statler Hotel regarding the admission of Negroes to all the meetings." Fred Dunn spoke on modern architecture, Rex Becker (of Froese, Maack & Becker) on traditional, and P. John Hoener on "Native American," by which he meant Colonial and Federal. Hoener underwrote part of the cost of the conference and arranged for the final dinner at Ladue Chapel, his 1949 design in the "Native American" style. A second conference on church architecture, held at the Chase in 1957, attracted 1,200 participants.

Other occasions for meetings grew out of the organization of the Missouri State Association of Registered Architects in 1951. Unlike the AIA, the MSARA (later the MARA) had a membership goal —all the registered architects in the state. Its first president was Harold A. Casey of Springfield, and early officers included St. Louisans Rex Becker, Robert Elkington, and Bennett Applegate. A couple of decades later the group was reorganized as the MCA—Missouri Council of Architects. In 1953, the association started its own magazine, *The Missouri Architect*. It was succeeded in 1972 by *The Midwest Architect*, which survived only through 1974.

A more important publication to St. Louis architects was the *Construction Record*, which appeared in the middle of 1954.

At first it was a monthly supplement to the *St. Louis Daily Record*, the legal newspaper that had been run since the 1890s by the Morse family. The *Construction Record* was conceived by publisher Lucius B. Morse and edited by Jack L. Theiss. The paper allotted special pages to all the construction-related organizations in the city, including, in addition to the

AIA, the Associated General Contractors, the Home Builders Association, the Missouri Society of Professional Engineers, the American Society of Heating, Refrigeration and Air-Conditioning Engineers, the Construction Specifications Institute, and the Producers Council.

Under the chairmanship of Edward J. Thias, whose office was in the same building as the *Daily Record*, the AIA got its section off to a splendid start. In contrast to the radio talks a generation earlier, the early issues of the "AIA Record" were lively, specific, and well-illustrated. They included a valuable series of biographical profiles of Chapter members, many of them written by close associates. Eugene Mackey, Jr., wrote about Joseph Murphy, for example, and the following year Murphy returned the favor.

Several architects had occasional columns, such as one by Kurt Landberg in the issue of July 1955, proposing the extension of the Civic Plaza mall from the Civil Courts Building to the Old Courthouse, with Market and Chestnut streets depressed. Doris Danna covered the Central States Regional Convention held in St. Louis in November of that year, and Betty Lou Custer later started a news-notes column, "Et Cetera." Jack Theiss purchased the *Construction Record* in the 1960s and moved its offices to Kirkwood, where it continued to be published until 1970.

In 1953 the Chamber of Commerce joined with the Chapter in cosponsoring the Merit Award Competition, to identify the best-designed buildings erected in the St. Louis area since 1941. Forty-eight entries by twenty-six firms were displayed at

Chapter President Lester C. Haeckel delivers awards of 1953 Merit Award Competition to gold medal certificate winners Harris Armstrong, *William T. Daly, George Hellmuth, and Joseph Murphy.*

The 1953 Merit Award Competition was judged by, from left, Samuel E. Homsey, *Richard M. Bennett, and former St. Louisan Hugh Ferriss.*

the City Art Museum for judging by Hugh Ferriss of New York, Richard M. Bennett of Chicago, and Samuel E. Homsey of Wilmington, Delaware. Five gold medal certificates and thirteen silver medal certificates were awarded at a ceremony November 9. Harris Armstrong won four of the eighteen prizes, including two of the top awards for his Lutheran Church of the Atonement in Florissant and his American Stove Company Building on South Kingshighway, one of the first and most innovative post-war office towers in the nation.

The Leo A. Daly Company, which had a St. Louis office but was based in Omaha, was recognized for the House of Philosophy at St. Louis University, later called the Fusz Memorial. The Cochran Apartments, whose design by Hellmuth, Yamasaki & Leinweber had been so vocally opposed by the Chapter, won also. Bennett declared, the *Post-Dispatch* reported, that such a project "would have cured many of Chicago's troubles and mounting problems of big cities in general today. . . . These apartments are well designed because they follow the scale of people, not that of vehicles or of merchandise." Joseph D. Murphy's design for St. Ann's Church in Normandy, done in partnership with Eugene J. Mackey, Jr., was praised in particular for Emil Frei's windows. Ferris extended to Frei the jury's "special acknowledgment in lieu of the windows' merited gold medal."

Emil Frei, Jr., (1896-1967) had long been recognized for his artistic achievements. An honorary associate of the St. Louis Chapter since 1943, he had worked for his father's art glass company (founded about 1900) since 1917 and had headed it since his father's death in 1942.

In earlier years, Emil Frei Art Glass was known first for its pictorial windows influenced by the Pre-Raphaelites and then for glass imitating Chartres, but after Robert Harmon joined the company in 1938, his modernistic and sometimes abstract designs drew national attention. In 1953, Frei received the Craftsmanship Medal that had been established in 1921 by the Institute. He was the first St. Louisan to receive any national AIA award.

The bond issue of 1955 was, at $110 million, even bigger than the famous 1923 bond issue. Civic Progress, the exclusive group of business leaders organized by Mayor Darst, adopted a slogan used by the *Post-Dispatch* to promote passage of the bond issue: "Progress or Decay." The centerpiece of the package of twenty-three propositions was the system of expressways (later designated U. S. 40, Interstate 55 and Interstate 70) intended to speed people downtown; only later did planners notice that these highways went both ways.

The AIA counted fifteen propositions that called for new architectural work worth over $30 million, including eight firehouses, four libraries, five buildings at the zoo, an auditorium for the art museum, a planetarium, a city workhouse, a voting machine warehouse, and improvements to nearly all the hospitals, other public buildings, and parks.

The Chapter was determined to make this work available to its members in private practice. Immediately after approval of the bond issue by overwhelming margins in May, the Chapter submitted a report to the city outlining procedures that could be used to select appropriate firms. The report included data from thirty-eight

Principals of one of the city's long-prominent firms in a rare photograph of them together in 1949. From left: E. J. Russell, William D. Crowell, Arthur F. Schwarz, Jr., and W. O. Mullgardt. The style of the firm then was Russell, Crowell, Mullgardt & Schwarz.

firms indicating their size and experience in projects of this sort, a portrait of the profession as it then was in St. Louis.

Excluding Leo A. Daly and Design Incorporated, which were not primarily local, the largest firm in terms of staff employed was Hellmuth, Obata & Kassabaum, which had been organized just that year. HOK had fifty employees, William B. Ittner forty-two, and Maguolo & Quick (the successors to O'Meara & Hills) thirty-three. Three firms had between twenty and thirty employees: Jamieson, Spearl, Hammond & Grolock; P. John Hoener & Associates; and Russell Mullgardt Schwarz Van Hoefen. That last, which as Mauran, Russell & Crowell had been the dominant firm in the city, was down from a high of 250 employees in 1942. A couple of other firms were doing a similar volume of work but with

fewer people: Marcel Boulicault and Kenneth Wischmeyer. By contrast, Harris Armstrong was operating with just four employees, and the most he had ever had was five.

The Chapter launched a new program in 1956 designed to give recognition to "the many skilled workmen in various crafts in the Metropolitan Area. It is felt that in this manner we can show appreciation for a job well done and also encourage the beginner to take greater pride in his work." Harris Armstrong chaired the committee, which worked with the Associated General Contractors to organize the awards into common categories of craftsmanship. Twelve men were selected for the first awards, presented at the January meeting. The response was so encouraging that the program was made annual.

Between-sessions conference at 1955 Central States Regional Convention, St. Louis. From left: Architect and planner Henry S. Churchill, principal speaker; Arthur F. Schwarz, Jr., Chapter president; Joseph D. Murphy, former dean of the Washington University School of Architecture; Albert Baum, St. Louis building commissioner; and Edward J. Thias, Chapter public relations chairman.

As the economy continued to improve, the Chapter grew in numbers and changed in composition. Institute Members, after 1954 called Corporate Members, once again outnumbered Associates, and by 1954 the total of all members was exactly twice what it had been in 1938: 240 from 120. At the same time, the old guard was rapidly thinning. After Mullgardt became emeritus in 1956, the Chapter had only one active fellow, Harris Armstrong, the apostle of modernism. He was joined the next year by Joseph D. Murphy.

With its larger membership, the Chapter could afford for the first time to hire an executive secretary and to rent an office. The executive committee met for the first time in the new office, Room H-18 of the Railway Exchange Building, on November 19, 1956. The minutes were taken by the new executive secretary, Esther Otto, the wife of Chapter member George Otto; she came in three days a week. Chapter members Syl G. Schmidt and Fred Paolinelli had their offices nearby in Room 1819, and Diedrich F. Rixmann was in Room 1822. The officers specified that all the furniture acquired for the new office was to be metal of gray finish. Early in 1957, Mrs. Otto was succeeded by Jean Schneeberger, the wife of member Nelson Schneeberger.

The American Institute of Architects celebrated its centennial in 1957. The St. Louis Chapter's Centennial Observance Committee, chaired by Joseph D. Mur-

Right: The Magic Chef Building, 1641 South Kingshighway, gold medal certificate winner for Harris Armstrong, 1953.

Below: Resurrection of Our Lord Catholic Church, 3900 Meramec Avenue, Murphy & Mackey. It placed fourth in the 1957 Chapter poll of the best buildings in St. Louis.

81 | New Technology

Right: George F. Hellmuth and a photo of controversial and later award-winning project by Hellmuth, Yamasaki & Leinweber, the John J. Cochran Garden Apartments.

Below: Lambert-St. Louis International (at that time Municipal) Airport Terminal, Hellmuth, Yamasaki & Leinweber, the first building in the St. Louis area to win a national AIA honor award, 1956.

phy, planned several commemorative events, including an exhibition, a major project, and a luncheon to be held one hundred years to the day after the founding of the Institute in New York on February 23, 1857.

For the exhibition, the Chapter asked its members to name the ten most signifi-

cant works of architecture in the community. The results reflected a profession that was proud of its accomplishments and confident of its direction. Of the forty buildings that received three or more votes, more than half were modern designs, all but two of them built in the previous decade.

Louis LaBeaume, for many years a dynamic influence in Chapter activities and in the community.

And while such national figures as Frank Lloyd Wright (the Russell Kraus house in Kirkwood) and Welton Beckett (Stix Westroads) received their due, most of the admired new work was by local firms. Kenneth Wischmeyer was cited for his deluxe supermarket at Clayton and Hanley roads, the first of its kind in this area. Four works by Harris Armstrong were nominated, topped by the American Stove Building. Joseph Murphy was represented by Faith Hospital on North Kingshighway, done with Angelo G. Corrubia, and by three buildings with Eugene Mackey. Their Resurrection Catholic Church on Meramec Street, parabolic in plan and furnished with Frei glass and other notable works of art, ranked fourth, ahead of the Old Courthouse, Eads Bridge, and Eric Mendelsohn's B'nai Amoona Synagogue in University City.

Like Murphy, George Hellmuth was also represented by two partnerships. The Bristol School in Webster Groves, one of the first commissions of his newly organized firm, Hellmuth, Obata & Kassabaum, placed tenth, and four projects by Hellmuth, Yamasaki & Leinweber were cited. Their terminal for the St. Louis municipal airport was at the top of the list, behind the Wainwright Building but just ahead of Union Station. It had won an AIA Honor Award the previous year, the first building in the area to be so

recognized. (In the years since, only the Arch, the Climatron, the Monsanto Company cafeteria, and the east wing remodeling of the St. Louis Art Museum have received national AIA awards.)

The exhibition at the Art Museum never took place because of budget constraints. The luncheon, however, came off splendidly. It was held in the Boulevard Room of the Hotel Jefferson, with the Chapter paying one-third of the cost and members the remaining $2 per person. John Bryan showed slides of the historic buildings in St. Louis that he considered most significant architecturally, and Louis LaBeaume, now the most senior member of the Chapter except for Will Levy (who had joined in 1901), reminisced about the St. Louis architectural scene since the 1890s.

LaBeaume's talk was subsequently published, first by the AIA as a pamphlet, *The Way We Came,* and then in the quarterly *Bulletin* of the Missouri Historical Society, as an article with the title, "Looking Backward at St. Louis Architecture." LaBeaume concluded his review by remarking that in modern architecture the past, instead of being merely prologue, was *kaput.* "The battle of the styles is over, but it is not yet safe to say that peace reigns either architecturally or politically. We have not quite waked up in St. Louis, but some of our architects are doing their best to rouse us."

The civic project the Chapter chose as a centennial offering to the city was an analysis of Saarinen's memorial design. The project had been stalled for nearly a decade by the difficulty of relocating the elevated tracks that ran along Wharf Street. Now a plan for tunneling the tracks through an artificial hill a few feet

Chapter officers, 1957: Hari Van Hoefen, director; Joseph Christie, treasurer; Roland Bockhorst, vice-president; Raymond Burns, *secretary; Eugene J. Mackey, Jr., president; Rex L. Becker, ex-officio; Gerhardt Kramer, director.*

In 1957, the Institute's Centennial year, the Chapter honored these members with thirty or more years of service: Fred Hammond, Ernest *Friton, Ray Leimkuehler, Paul Valenti, P. J. Hoener, and Ewald Froese.*

from their original location gave new hope for completion of the project in time for the city's two-hundredth birthday in 1964.

Eric Smith, chairman of the Projects Committee, stressed the importance of this in a four-page essay in the April 1957 inaugural issue of the new Chapter *Newsletter,* intended to supplement the AIA section of the *Construction Record.* Smith encouraged the Chapter to formulate a formal endorsement for Saarinen's design for the Jefferson National Expansion Memorial. The Chapter could, he said, "serve as a catalyst to bring the JNEM into reality. . . . Those who want to see this project materialize (and this committee certainly does) must raise a tremendous voice in its behalf."

Smith and Chapter President Eugene J. Mackey, Jr., did exactly that, speaking to every group that would hear them and inducing the major newspapers to run dozens of articles on the issue. Dean Joseph R. Passonneau of the Washington University School of Architecture later wrote that "the St. Louis architects convinced people that the quality of the design in itself made the project worth doing and that this was decisive in getting the job done."

At the end of the year, Mackey spoke from personal experience when he challenged Chapter members to take greater responsibility in public affairs: "No city is built great without abundant civic pride—and civic pride is the child of civic participation. Though the price is high, we can afford no less if we are to achieve a distinguished city worthy of a second centennial."

Detail, Columbia Brewery, Madison and North Twentieth, 1892. E. Jungenfeld & Co. Listed National Register of Historic Places, 1984.

Pat Hays Baer, for Landmarks Association of St. Louis

The first Architects' Sunday tour, December 1970. These tours of new and old architecture comprise the Chapter's most sustained and successful program for bringing architects, architecture, and the public into conversational contact. For the first tour, Harris Armstrong (far right), led visitors through his Ethical Society Meeting House, Clayton.

III

The Architect in Public

By Mary Henderson Gass

10
Out of the Cloister

To state the condition in its simplest
terms—if adequate measures are not
taken, the city is faced with gradual
economic and social collapse. The old
central areas of the city are being
abandoned and this insidious trend
will continue until the entire city is
engulfed.
—"Urban Land Policy, St.
Louis Missouri," City Plan
Commission, 1936

THE SOMBER WARNING was issued at
the midpoint of the Great Depression, and
then came World War II. Construction
had been close to a standstill during the
budget-starved years of hard times, and
building materials were under military
priorities during the war.

The decade after the war was a time of
catch-up renovation and repair. The glory
days of stately commercial edifices, to
which Ecole des Beaux Arts training had
contributed so abundantly along
Washington Avenue and other St. Louis
streets, were history. Soon, much of the
city would have to be revitalized with new
construction and new uses of existing
buildings, and architects and the public
would begin to meet and to know each

other better than most of them ever had
before.

A Chamber of Commerce survey of
construction in the central business district
between 1930 and 1957 reported that in
those decades only fourteen buildings had
gone up. Twelve were for retail space and
two for offices, none significant to the
downtownness of downtown. The survey
noted that seventy-five percent of the core
buildings were more than fifty years old.

From the 1957 point of view, senior
buildings were candidates for replacement
according to calculations based on age,
condition, tenancy, and potential alternative uses of their sites. The potential
might be a new building eventually but a
parking lot immediately, with modest

parking fees and tax savings incentives enough for demolition. A factor hardly ever in the equation was architectural merit.

Two authorities on merit were John Albury Bryan, whose knowledge of the heritage of downtown buildings and their architects was encyclopedic, and Buford L. Pickens, dean of the School of Architecture, Washington University, who taught architectural history. They spoke up when important buildings were threatened, but the advice most heeded at the command level was from authorities in short-term economics. Some demolition was an accomplished fact before the landmark quality of a building could be considered, or on such short notice as to preclude research.

Newspaper reports of buildings on the way to a dump often quoted Dr. William G. Swekosky, who emerged as a sort of default authority and usually was identified as "a dentist whose hobby is old buildings." Dr. Swekosky devoted spare time to combing city records, and when a building was about to vanish he would write or telephone the papers with information about its age and original ownership. With luck, the papers might get a photographer on the scene while the ruin was still recognizable.

The interested party least likely to be consulted about anything done downtown was the body of city residents, the public. Its stake in the quality of its community was high, but with initiatives managed by on-the-spot business and political leadership, the public seldom volunteered any observations. One foreboding reason was that much of the public was no longer there, having switched from former in-town haunts to suburban equivalents with free and easy parking.

A citizen generation had grown up with no particular attitudes toward the planning and design of its city—that had always been left to the experts. The public's attention was invited to such matters when its vote was needed on tax proposals or bond issues. It was when city-wide construction was resumed under federal urban renewal that the citizenry suddenly had a direct financial stake in most major projects, public and private—a huge participation.

The ceremonial thrust of a shovel into the dirt of a construction site hardly ever took place without support from tax funds or tax abatements, or both. As the de-facto partner in land-clearance and redevelopment projects, the public had an interest in knowing how well its money was being used not only for physical inventory but also for economic, social, and cultural advantage. Usually, the public partner was given meager, project-promotional information.

In a community hungry for progress, post-war priorities were primarily fixed on the downtown core, with its vacated offices, postponed upgrading, and parking lots marking the spots where buildings had been convicted of obsolescence and executed. The most heartening and convincing signs of progress and new life were excavation barriers, pile drivers, ascending steel frames, towering cranes, mortar mixers, and swarms of bricklayers. The need to replenish and expand also energized outlying neighborhoods and the rapidly expanding suburbia.

St. Louis architects entered the 1950s with expectations of major roles in the revival of their long-neglected city. They found, however, that architectural design had become generally perceived more as

Mayor Raymond R. Tucker signing proclamation for Architects' Week, 1959, flanked by Lester Roth (left) and Gerhardt Kramer.

concerns had attentive audiences. Broadened conceptions of humane urban environments were explored in monthly Monday evening talks and forums in Washington University's Givens Hall by local speakers and visiting authorities, often with newspaper coverage. The public was invited. Dean Joseph R. Passonneau of the School of Architecture, who set an example of the architect as an urban philosopher, argued in talks and writings that well-conceived architecture could actually help to generate creative activities.

During Gerhardt Kramer's term as president (1958), the Chapter established several programs to educate the public in issues of architectural design, along with discreet promotion of members' current projects in exhibitions of drawings and photographs. Through a speakers bureau that coped with the ivory-tower stereotype and helped members to become more articulate in public forums, many of the public met an architect for the first time. Films and slides enhanced these presentations, and by 1967 the Chapter was sponsoring six a month.

Kramer also instituted Architects' Week, which became so popular that it was repeated annually into the early 1970s. These programs and exhibitions were meant, he said, "to infuse an appreciation of the art of architecture in the minds of the millions of people who reside in our metropolitan area. We realize this cannot be done in a week—but maybe after a year, or 10 years, or 100 years [he was willing to persist!] the people will have developed an appreciation to such a degree that they will demand better architecture and reject inferior design."

The Chapter extended its orbit in 1959 with "Progress Through Architecture

skin-deep embellishment, an optional extra, than as the means of making buildings work well for their occupants and for the cityscape. Many clients, most of the public, and some architects were talking more about bricks and mortar than about felicitous and harmonious design, and the AIA ruefully acknowledged in national convention programs that the profession offered few influential examples of the ideals that it claimed to represent.

Architects' discussions turned to the larger issues of urban spaces, and to the whole environment, natural and man-made. "Environment" became an emphasized word in program agendas, and speakers and writers who addressed such

Eero Saarinen, architect of the Gateway Arch (center) visited St. Louis March 10, 1959, for a ceremony at the Old Courthouse in which Mayor Tucker (right) delivered the city's share of first-phase financing. George Hartzog, then superintendent of the yet-to-come Jefferson National Expansion Memorial is at left.

Week'' and a new *Yearbook*—2,000 copies—to showcase projects by some thirty members, together with the full membership roster and the current fee schedule. The event included exhibitions and tours of offices and residences of Chapter members, awards ceremonies, and member participation in four television and two radio programs.

One of the tour offices was that of the fledgling firm, Hellmuth Obata & Kassabaum, at 315 North Tenth Street; others were the work rooms of Murphy & Mackey, 6124 Enright Avenue; Kramer & Harms, 9640 Clayton Road (a converted gas station); Rathert & Roth, 4401 Hampton Avenue; and Harris Armstrong, whose elegantly reticent office, near his house in Kirkwood, was accessed via a handsomely crafted bridge over a lily pond. The residences of William B. Ittner,

Edward J. Thias, and Bernard McMahon also were on the tours.

A Chapter exhibition at the Old Courthouse combined drawings and watercolor renderings of historic landmarks with models and photographs of members' projects. It also called attention to the building itself as a milestone in St. Louis architecture. In conjunction with Washington University, the Central Public Library exhibited rare architectural books.

The week's culmination was a joint AIA-Producers' Council dinner at the Starlight Roof of the Chase Hotel, at which Charles Van Ravenswaay, director of the Missouri Historical Society, and George McCue, art and urban design critic of the *Post-Dispatch,* were made honorary associates of the Chapter. McCue had just been awarded, for the second time, the national AIA first prize of $500 for excellence in architectural journalism. The organizers of the week's events, headed by Lester Roth, were Rex Becker, Betty Lou Custer, Frederick C. Sternberg, Hari Van Hoefen, Joseph D. Murphy, and Donald Porter Wilson.

The success of this intensive exposure was indicated both by its focusing of public attention on the profession and by two student programs that grew out of it—the Scholarship Fund and the annual High School Drafting Competition. The former, instituted with $500 profit from the tours, was enlarged by ensuing tours, by Women's Architectural League events, and finally by the $2,500 profit from the 1964 national convention in St. Louis, all put into a trust for aid to future architects.

The first winners of the drafting competition, organized by John Sweeney, received certificates on an Architects' Week television program. In 1967 the competition was extended to students of junior colleges and technical schools, with modest cash prizes. Each year the winners, with their parents and teachers, were guests at the Chapter's May dinner meeting for programs typically about architectural education. Deans George Anselevicius and Constantine Michaelides were among the speakers.

Rosary High School teacher Eugene Schnell became a regular guest at these affairs—in 1971, a *Post-Dispatch* headline announced: "Rosary Wins All High School Drafting Awards for the 4th Year in Row." In 1974 the competition was broadened to include photography, rendering, and model-building, and in 1976 there were 109 entries. The Chapter exhibited award work at its office for a

month. Prize-winners who became architects and Chapter members included Howard Koblenz (1960), Anthony J. Amato, Jr. (1962), Ronald M. Reim and Bryan E. Sechrist (1977), and Cynthia E. Easterling (1978). This program had a long run—until 1984.

One of Gerhardt Kramer's last major achievements as president was to lead a delegation to the Octagon to make the case for St. Louis as the AIA national convention site for 1964—the city's bicentennial year. The Chapter was awarded that massive commitment, and since members' wives were tacitly enlisted for the Chapter's major enterprises anyway, a considerable number of them made their support roles more specific through the Women's Architectural League, organized by Louise (Mrs. Harris) Armstrong in November 1960. The WAL was introduced in the 1961 *Yearbook* as the "Auxiliary to the St. Louis Chapter, AIA," and it remained a stalwart and resourceful ally.

The WAL began with eighty-eight Chapter wives and eight honorary members under Mrs. Armstrong as president. Her husband was then Chapter president, and other WAL leaders were the wives of Chapter officers and past presidents: Mary (Mrs. Eugene) Mackey, Jr., Tena (Mrs. Lester) Roth, Maxine (Mrs. Robert) Elkington, Bernice (Mrs. Arthur) Schwarz, Ravenna (Mrs. Gerhardt) Kramer, Frances (Mrs. Frederick C.) Sternberg, Ada (Mrs. Rex L.) Becker, Marjory (Mrs. George E.) Kassabaum, Micki (Mrs. Eric W.) Smith, Mary (Mrs. W. Evans) Campbell, Bernice (Mrs. Chester E.) Roemer, Pat (Mrs. King) Graf, and Ann (Mrs. Joseph D.) Murphy.

Betty Lou Custer, a 1944 graduate of the Washington University School of Architecture and licensed in Missouri in 1949, was both a Chapter member and an officer in the WAL. Other WAL members who were architects and Chapter members were also spouses of architects: Doris (Mrs. Charles) Danna, Susan Sallee (Mrs. Charles W.) Lorenz, and Mary Jane (Mrs. Ralph A.) Fournier.

In 1960, under president Frederick C. Sternberg, the Chapter planned the second annual Architects' Week around the two-day annual convention of the Missouri Association of Registered Architects in May at the Park Plaza Hotel. John Sweeney, MARA president, arranged for welcoming ceremonies in the new Steinberg Hall on the Washington University campus, with Dean Passonneau as speaker. The building, given by Mrs. Mark C. Steinberg, was one of the earliest projects of Fumihiko Maki, a visiting professor at the School of Architecture from 1956 to 1963. Maki, destined for international acclaim, was not licensed in Missouri, and Russell Mullgardt Schwarz Van Hoefen served as the associated architects for this project.

In the same week, the Chapter and guests previewed another innovative structure, the Climatron, at its monthly dinner meeting at the Missouri Botanical Garden. The following spring, the geodesic dome greenhouse made its architects, Murphy & Mackey, the first American firm to win the $25,000 R. S. Reynolds Memorial Award, administered by the AIA, for significant architectural use of aluminum. (In 1988, Maki would receive the same prize for his Spiral Building in Tokyo.)

Rex Becker, chairman of Architects' Week in 1960, assigned the *Yearbook* pro-duction to William Bodley Lane. Besides double-page spreads of members' new projects, the book featured pencil sketches by W. Evans Campbell and Ralph A. Fournier of sixteen houses opened to public tours. The tours were organized by Betty Lou Custer and the WAL to benefit the Scholarship Fund. A falling-off of support for the *Yearbook* made the third edition of 1961 the last to be published.

Architects' Week, however, was another success, associated this time with the Sixteenth Central States Conference September 28-30 at the Sheraton Jefferson Hotel. The scheduling of Edward D. Stone as speaker assured a full turnout, and the prominent New York architect, articulate and outspoken, lived up to expectations. Stone urged the architects of the central region to "go to bat for beauty," because "in the last thirty or forty years we have succeeded in converting [this country] from the most beautiful country in the world to one of the ugliest."

Stone had delivered the same speech the year before at the National Conference of Editorial Writers at Richmond, Virginia, and one of its apothegms was widely quoted: "An English observer visiting this country said that he noticed a firm determination on our part to pave our country with car lots, beer cans, billboards, and Bar-B-Q's in order that we might whiz by in a lemon-yellow Cadillac with a platinum blonde and contemplate the ruins in style."

Stone's visit and his acerbic message coincided with public debate over design proposals by Sverdrup & Parcel for the downtown stadium. In an August 7 guest editorial in the *Post-Dispatch,* Chapter president Harris Armstrong called for an

In 1962, Mayor Tucker cut the ribbon for the Chapter's move into commodious office space and exhibition gallery at 1126 Locust Street, and members saluted prospects of enlarged public awareness of urban design. William Rupe and Angelo Corrubia are at left, President John David Sweeney at right.

outside design review panel for this project. He wrote: "The best approach of course would be to engage a great designer and put him in charge, give him authority and make him responsible. . . . I wish to make it quite clear that this is in no sense a criticism [of Sverdrup & Parcel]; but the actual control of the project is, I fear, in other hands."

Armstrong suggested Pier Luigi Nervi as a possible designer. On a trip to New York shortly afterward, Mayor Raymond R. Tucker had a chat with Stone about the stadium. At the suggestion of Howard Baer, the Civic Center Redevelopment Corporation, the owner, selected Stone as design collaborator with Sverdrup & Parcel for the stadium exterior, with Schwarz & Van Hoefen as associates.

Delegates to the Central States Conference were keenly interested in two projects then under construction—the HOK Planetarium in Forest Park and Eero Saarinen's Gateway Arch. They remarked on demolition in the Mill Creek Valley redevelopment, some with admiration of the vistas of downtown that it opened, and others with misgivings about the totality of the 454-acre clearance. The delegates and St. Louis residents toured contemporary houses by Harris Armstrong; John A. Grunik; Dunn & Stinson; Wedemeyer &

Hecker; Bernoudy, Mutrux & Bauer; Hellmuth Obata & Kassabaum; Walter B. Kromm; and Froese, Maack & Becker.

A matter of profound concern to architects, builders, construction unions, and clientele late in 1960 was the substantial revision of the 1945 building code being considered by the St. Louis Board of Aldermen. Proposed revisions took cognizance of new materials and technology, and inaugurated criteria of performance rather than of specified materials.

Debate became heated over a provision to allow metal panel and masonry veneer curtain walls without backup masonry. Architects and clients of business projects in particular regarded this change as crucial to the city's progress, the existing code having already driven some construction into more progressive suburbs. Other traditional standards regarded as obsolete affected electrical and plumbing installations. Chapter spokesmen argued vigorously for the new code. Two firms, HOK and Harris Armstrong, obviously had bet on its passage, for panels of colored, unbacked porcelain soon blossomed prominently in their Plaza Square Apartments, in blocks adjacent to Memorial Plaza.

At that time, the executive committee under Armstrong was looking for a new Chapter office location with better public visibility and larger space for meetings to plan the convention. A decision to remain downtown followed a survey showing that the offices of twenty-four firms were in or near the core. The committee favored ground-floor space in the Arcade Building, but the membership balked at the expense.

In 1962 with John Sweeney as president, the Chapter became intrigued with the idea of establishing an ''Architectural Center'' in the Columbian Building at 1126 Locust Street—a big order, for the Chapter would have to buy the seven-story building and renovate it for its own and tenant space. Originally designed as the Town Club by Mauran, Russell & Crowell, with a basement swimming pool and a restaurant, it had been used by a women's organization until the depression. Then it had served as the Columbian Club, a businessmen's gathering place, until the club disbanded in 1957.

The Architectural Center role model was an Atlanta Chapter facility, which accommodated the AIA, the WAL, and the Producers' Council, including space for product exhibitions. Verner Burks was asked to draw plans for similar use of the Columbian Building, and in the meantime the Chapter leased half the ground floor.

In July 1962 Mayor Tucker cut the ribbon to dedicate the new headquarters. The Chapter paid $125 a month in rent, and spent approximately $4,500 for renovation with air-conditioning and new furnishings. Members helped with painting and carpentry. The architectural showcase dream faded while the Chapter went ahead with more manageable use of the office as a public information center with an exhibition gallery. Information about member firms was made available, and visitors had access to a library and a coffee bar.

It was for this office that Angelo G. Corrubia, son of the respectfully remembered Angelo B. M. Corrubia, designed the round conference table; the bentwood chairs still in use were acquired to go with it.

The Jefferson National Expansion Memorial site as seen by delegates to the 1964 national AIA convention— legs of the Gateway Arch entering the skyline, depressed interstate highways under construction next to the Old Cathedral, construction sheds scattered over the future park area.

11
Convention City / Urban Renewal: 1964

To BE READY for its first national convention since 1928, the Chapter would need every day of the five-year lead time. What had begun as men-only conclaves that would fit into one room had grown into great gatherings of members and spouses, all renewing old acquaintance, choosing among many program options, spreading over the host city to check out its exemplary architecture and other attractions, and hearing speakers who often could be counted on to probe vulnerable areas of the profession for raw nerves.

Planning for the convention built up the momentum of Chapter activities and spurred attendance at monthly meetings. The meetings adhered to the agreeable format of drinks, dinner, business, and a program, rotated among tried and proved restaurants. The Cheshire Inn was highly favored, but members also met and dined at the Gatesworth Hotel, Kemoll's, the Flaming Pit, the Crest House, and John Henry's Railroad Restaurant in Northwest Plaza. Secretary William Bodley Lane time-capsuled the dishes served to seventy-three members at a post-convention dinner

on October 27, 1964, at the Louis IX Room, Union Station: "Breaded veal cutlet, potatoes, peas and chef's salad with a desert of cherries jubilee"—at $3.50 a plate.

Programs with special emphasis were held in certain months, with the craftsmanship awards in September and the drafting awards in May. June, the Summer Party month, also had been the month for officer installations, the terms running from July through June, with elections in May. In 1963, however, an Octagon mandate shifted the terms to the calendar year. The first president installed within the new time frame was George E. Kassabaum, in December 1963, with 103 persons filling the room at what was then the Bel Air Motor Hotel, at Lindell and Euclid. That put Kassabaum at the throttle for the national convention, and on the track to the national presidency four years later.

The convention was held at the Chase Park Plaza June 14-17, 1964. As host, the Chapter organized all the sightseeing and entertainment events and managed the

Judging of student drafting competition entries, 1964. From left, Lester C. Haeckel, W. Evans *Campbell, Erwin Carl Schmidt.*

myriad logistical details of this meeting of 2,486 delegates. George Hellmuth and Eugene Mackey, Jr., moderated workshops in the professional program, its theme, ''The City Visible and Invisible.'' Mayor Raymond R. Tucker, Honorary AIA, and Thomas Eliot, chancellor of Washington University, spoke on the legal structure and organization of cities.

Records attest to that convention's notable success and to the Chapter's standard-setting hospitality. More than 140 Chapter members—nearly half the roster—were joined by WAL members in the corps of volunteers for countless tasks. Joseph Murphy was chairman of the steering committee, which included Rex Becker, Betty Lou Custer, John Sweeney,

and George Kassabaum.

Guests from other chapters praised the programs for their comprehensive exposures of St. Louis architecture and for events in a broad range of serious-to-fun preferences. They included a walking tour of five houses on Portland and Westmoreland places, bus tours of old and new St. Louis, and children's tours. There were a night at the Muny, a party at the Zoo, films on St. Louis and the Gateway Arch (then rising from its footings), an organ recital at the St. Louis Cathedral, a reception for women architects, and a WAL champagne brunch at the University Club for 225 guests, at which AIA wives modeled period costumes in a program, ''The St. Louis Woman from 1764 to

In advance of the 1964 St. Louis convention, the river-city spirit was evoked in photo tableau in the Missouri Historical Society Museum. Chapter President George Kassabaum is in the pilothouse with Doris Ittner who, with *Doris Danna (on steps), chaired social events; Joseph D. Murphy, seated, was convention chairman. The Danna children, Paul and Susan, and their mother wore period costumes.*

1964.''

The principal events were a party at Grant's Farm and the Chapter party, ''Evening on the Mississippi,'' a riverboat excursion heralded by a steam calliope, with dinner and dancing. Doris and H. Curtis Ittner were in charge of the voyage, and other activities were organized by Harris Armstrong, Betty Lou Custer, Theodore J. Wofford, Gerhardt

Kramer, Bee Freeman, W. Allen Cleneay, Robert Entzeroth, and John Sweeney. Earl A. Fey and Edward Dieckmann were in charge of bus transportation, and Nolan L. Stinson, Jr., organized the hospitality lounge.

In timing with the convention, the City Art Museum dedicated five galleries to a month-long exhibition, designed by Eric W. Smith, Jr., and William Peckham, of

St. Louisans advanced to rank of Fellow at 1964 convention: Dean Joseph R. Passoneau, Eric W. Smith, Jr., Hari Van Hoefen, and Eugene J. Mackey, Jr. At right is Arthur Gould Odell, Jr., newly installed president of the Institute.

160 large black-and-white photographs of structures designed by recipients of the AIA Gold Medal—Pier Luigi Nervi, Alvar Aalto, Eero Saarinen, Le Corbusier, and Mies van der Rohe. Nervi, who was to receive the Gold Medal at the banquet on the following evening, was acclaimed at the opening reception, attended by 2,000 people.

Four St. Louisans were advanced to the rank of Fellow at the banquet: Eugene J. Mackey, Jr., for collaboration in the design of the Climatron and for expediting construction of the Jefferson National Expansion Memorial; Dean Joseph R. Passonneau of the Washington University School of Architecture for education; Eric W. Smith, Jr., for design of the Gaylord Music Library, Washington University, and other projects; and Hari Van Hoefen, for service to the profession as member of the Missouri Board of Registration for Architects and Engineers, and of the National Architectural Accrediting Board.

George McCue, arts editor of the *Post-Dispatch,* was made an honorary member of the Institute. He was author of *The Building Art in St. Louis: Two Centuries,* a ninety-six-page guidebook produced for the convention. Buford L. Pickens wrote the introduction, and a committee headed by Robert Elkington selected the entries. Enlarged editions of this book were published in 1967 and 1981, and it became the standard reference for architectural information about St. Louis.

Visitors to the city in 1964 saw it in a state of radical transformation—the Gateway Arch and the Mansion House complex under construction on the riverfront, the stadium site ready for clearance and construction, more than 400 bulldozed acres in Mill Creek Valley in the state of devastation that gave it the name, "Hiroshima Flats."

A report by Ada Louise Huxtable in *The New York Times* was headed "St. Louis Tears Itself Apart." "While the architects discussed the forces that shape cities in their professional programs, they saw a city that has more shapeless, bulldozed open space and more ambitious and debatable plans for renewal than almost any other in the country," she wrote, and called for more professional planning.

Regarding the city's proposal to raze thirty more blocks of downtown for the stadium and parking facilities, Huxtable questioned that a "Downtown for Cars is synonymous with a Downtown for People,

particularly when no provisions are being made for pedestrian pleasures." She urged the city to preserve its historical landmarks, such as the Wainwright Building and Union Station. She praised the AIA for a resolution supporting preservation of the Old Post Office, then in danger of demolition for a proposed Federal office tower in a public plaza.

The AIA convention resolution, formulated by the St. Louis Chapter, was instrumental in elevating the Old Post Office preservation campaign from a local to a national issue. It temporarily halted demolition plans and influenced the General Services Administration's consideration of adaptive reuse. It also was a turning point in the Chapter's preservation philosophy.

12
New Look at Old Architecture

THE CHAPTER HAD BEEN AMBIVALENT about the Old Post Office issue for a long time because of divided sentiments among its members, many of whom favored the tower and plaza concept for the Old Post Office block, as well as the city's demolish-and-replace urban renewal programs. Early in 1959, Harris Armstrong had proposed closing twenty-four core blocks for pedestrian malls, putting elevated moving sidewalks between huge parking structures north and south of the core, and replacing the Old Post Office with a landscaped civic center. In 1961 the Chapter had passed a resolution favoring OPO preservation only if the government could find an economically feasible use for the building.

Some weeks after the 1964 convention, a delegation of Chapter members and other citizens traveled to Washington with a rather desperate plan, prepared by William Peckham, for gaining office space that the Federal government deemed it needed by inserting intermediate floors within the tall-ceilinged building and adding three setback stories.

The group was led by Austin P. Leland, a St. Louis businessman and trustee of the National Trust for Historic Preservation. Others were Verner Burks, president of the Landmarks Association of St. Louis and chairman of the Old Post Office Landmarks Committee; George Kassabaum, Chapter president; Dean Joseph Passonneau; and Joseph Murphy. The General Services Administration rejected the plan because its modern interior deviated from "authentic historic preservation."

Finally, Congress broke a long impasse with what became known as the Old Post Office Act, which permitted combined Federal and commercial uses and liberated many another Federal property from all-or-nothing bondage. In a GSA competition to restore the building, two St. Louis firms were finalists—William B. Ittner, Inc., with Kaplan-McLaughlin of San Francisco, and Eugene J. Mackey [III] & Associates, with Anderson Notter Finegold of Boston. The winning team was Patty, Berkebile, Nelson Associates of Kansas City, with Harry Weese & Associates of

Chicago. The building was opened in 1978 with upper-story federal offices and commercial space in lower levels.

The post-war strategy for dealing with truly awful slums and with advanced decay in other older parts was clean-sweep riddance and rebuilding for the aura of newness. Some architecture of historic merit was caught in the purge. Some new construction lived up to concept renderings of open spaces, trees, strollways, and engaging facades. Mill Creek Valley acquired well-conceived moderate-income housing, but south of Market Street development fell markedly short of the industrial-park character that had been projected.

Some of the social assumptions of urban renewal proved to be grievously wrong. The relocation of dispossessed Mill Creek families overloaded other neighborhoods and created new blight. Public housing projects—the notoriously flawed Pruitt-Igoe complex only one among several—put former slum families in multi-story housing to which many never became adjusted. Valuable resources in the cultural heritage were broomed away.

Historic buildings and places were vulnerable at every level of urban renewal. Clean-slate developers did not want to plan around existing buildings; renewal conceptualizers were not accustomed to thinking about old properties as marketable and ornamental anchor points within radically changed neighborhoods; many architects had only light grounding in the history of their art and had no experience in recapturing old forms and patinas; nineteenth-century techniques of joinery, masonry, plaster ornament, and hardware had all but disappeared from artisans' vocabularies.

Some preservationists weakened their cases by holding to the idea that their calling was more to identify buildings for others to enshrine than to help devise adaptive new uses. Critical writing about architecture, urban design, and preservation appeared mainly on editorial pages, where uncertainties abounded.

Meanwhile, John Bryan and his committee on Preservation of Historic Buildings existed as a sort of active underground. When Mayor Raymond R. Tucker asked for identification of significant buildings and sites in 1964, Bryan and his committee marked forty of them on a map that was published in the *Post-Dispatch*. A 1967 edition of the map ventured sixty-two listings.

The St. Louis Landmarks and Urban Design Commission, a municipal agency to initiate protection policies for buildings of historic and architectural value, was established in 1965, but, like the predecessor Municipal Art Commission, with authority largely limited to moral suasion. The Chapter preservation committee, associated with the national AIA committee of equivalent objectives, gradually won credence—under Bryan until 1962, and then under Buford Pickens, Richard Bliss, W. Philip Cotton, Jr., and Theodore Wofford. Long-standing members were Gerhardt Kramer, Verner Burks, William Bodley Lane, and John Schulte.

Urban renewal was both the demon that devoured historic buildings and the catalyst of preservation. Developers needed to know about sensitive properties before point-of-no-return commitments, and preservationists needed research to support their pleadings. Grassfire crises kept catching both sides off balance. Information apparatus already existed, and the crises accelerated the research.

The organization that grew into the prime resource was the Landmarks Association of St. Louis, Inc., founded in 1958 with Joseph Passonneau as president. It was born in crisis—the Mark Twain Expressway threat to undercut the steep slope crowned by the Lewis Bissell Mansion near Grand Avenue. Landmarks devised a retaining wall that served both house and highway, and immediately turned to the rescue of the Chatillon-DeMenil House from a ramp of Interstate 55.

Landmarks became the vigilant sentinel, the keeper of quickly available files to aid judgments of new and historic options, and often the originator of resourceful solutions to having it both ways. Its particular value has been attention to properties of local and regional importance, and, ahead of their national recognition, to unique vernacular styles. Verner Burks and Gerhardt Kramer served subsequently as presidents, and the Chapter found itself in and out of accord with Landmarks in a stream of confrontational issues, especially those affecting downtown buildings.

By 1963 the Historic American Buildings Survey had recorded some 10,000 buildings nationwide. Peterson, who founded HABS in 1933, came to St. Louis to head the field office for the recording of riverfront buildings to be demolished for the Jefferson National Expansion Memorial. He employed John A. Bryan for research, and the writings of both became the basis of St. Louis documentation. The HABS studies, established in collaboration with the AIA and the Library of Congress, were begun in the depression by unemployed ar-

chitects and draftsmen with relief funds under the Civil Works Administration.

In 1949 the National Trust for Historic Preservation, a quasi-public organization not a part of the federal government but chartered by congress, began to acquire and preserve historic properties and to encourage the public in preservation practices. The Trust was organized in the board room of the Octagon, headquarters of the American Institute of Architects, where its offices remained for a year.

In 1966 the Historic Sites Act authorized the Secretary of the Interior to maintain a national register of sites, buildings, and other entities significant in American history and culture. The first published edition of the Register, prepared by the National Park Service in 1969, contained more than a thousand entries. Its frontispiece was a photograph of the Italianate stone Benoist House, "Oakland," in Affton, c.1854, by George I. Barnett. The 1966 Historic Preservation Act offered federal aid to state programs for recording and preservation, and opened the National Register to state listings. Its Missouri liaison now is the Division of Parks, Recreation and Historic Preservation under the Department of Natural Resources.

When the Columbian Club Building was demolished for a parking structure in 1965, the Chapter again took a significant position in historic preservation by moving its office to the Wainwright Building, then close to demolition for parking space. President Kassabaum pointed out that Louis Sullivan's distinguished design "represents a link between today's high-rise cities and architecture of the past." The Chapter established itself in a shop-front space facing Seventh Street, and

Delegates to the 1965 national convention, Washington, D.C., at the Chapter's much-used round table: standing: Ralph A. Fournier, Rex L. Becker, Eric W. Smith, Jr., Robert E. Haldiman, Chester E.

Roemer, Chapter President George E. Kassabaum, and William W. Rupe. Seated: John D. Sweeney, Nettie Bacle, Robert Elkington, Executive Secretary Jean Schneeberger, Kurt Landberg, and Maurice Johansen.

At a dinner-dance celebration of the Chapter's seventy-fifth anniversary, twelve past presidents were honored. Standing: Angelo Corrubia, George Kassabaum, Eugene J. Mackey, Jr., John Sweeney, Frederick Sternberg,

Gerhardt Kramer, and Rex Becker. Seated: Robert Elkington, Harris Armstrong, P. John Hoener, Fred Hammond, Joseph D. Murphy.

St. Louisans advanced to rank of Fellow in 1967: Rex L. Becker, George E. Kassabaum, Buford L. Pickens, Charles E. King.

Mayor Alfonso J. Cervantes cut the dedication ribbon on June 5, 1966. An exhibition of Sullivan designs, the first in the new gallery space, emphasized the historical importance of the architect and his famous St. Louis building.

The round conference table had to be cut down by almost two feet for the tighter new quarters. Member services were expanded, under Kenneth Schaefer's supervision, to include the sale of AIA documents and forms, a time-saving convenience.

The Women's Architectural League took a substantial initiative in public architectural education. Heeding pleas from teachers for reliable reference material, it published, in 1969, *Architecture in St. Louis: Twelve Historic Structures* and *Architecture in St. Louis: Twelve Contemporary Buildings.* Both were researched by the WAL Education Committee, the first under the direction of Hylarie (Mrs. William P.) McMahon, the other under Micki (Mrs. Eric W.) Smith.

Medallion relief, Edward G. Garden residence, 23 Windemere Place, 1907. Architects: Mauran, Russell & Garden.

13

The Gateway Mall

FOLLOWING THE TRIUMPHANT completion of the Gateway Arch in 1965, the city revived an idea advanced in 1951 by the City Plan Commission for making the blocks along the axis of the Gateway Arch, between Market and Chestnut streets, into a civic corridor. The idea was enthusiastically endorsed by Downtown St. Louis, Inc., organized in 1957 to promote core development.

The vision of linkage with existing landscaped blocks into a continuous strip was designated the Gateway Mall, beginning with the Gateway Arch itself, in the Jefferson National Expansion Memorial. Blocks already landscaped were Luther Ely Smith Park, east of the Old Courthouse, and Broadway-to-Sixth Kiener Plaza, a much-used brown-bag-lunch green with a fountain and the sculpture, *Olympic Runner*. Between Sixth and Eleventh were a parking lot and a mix of ordinary commercial and several landmark office buildings. Past Civil Courts, west of Twelfth (now Tucker) Boulevard, were Memorial Plaza and finally Aloe Plaza, with the renowned Carl Milles fountain, *Meeting of the Waters*.

The western terminus was at Twenty-first Street. Elements in place represented partial implementation of the City Plan Commission's 1912 Central Traffic-Parkway scheme, which proposed green blocks between Twelfth Street and Grand Avenue.

Over the years, three Chapter members had roles in these developments, all in the firm that began as Mauran, Russell & Garden. John Lawrence Mauran took part in the Civic League's drafting of the first comprehensive city plan of 1907. Later, Ernest John Russell became a member of the City Plan Commission and its chairman from 1917 to 1937, heading it again during 1944. When he resigned from the Commission in 1949, Mayor Aloys P. Kaufmann appointed Arthur F. Schwarz, Jr., to succeed him.

Starting with Mauran, Russell & Crowell as an office boy in 1927, Schwarz took night courses at Washington University, became an associate of Mauran, Russell, Crowell & Mullgardt, and later design architect for the City Plan Commission. He rejoined the firm in 1947, was Chapter president in 1955, and in

1958 was elected plan commission chairman. He also served for several years as chairman of the Downtown St. Louis, Inc., planning committee.

In 1958, Schwarz, wearing two hats as chairman of the Downtown, Inc., planning committee and chairman of the City Plan Commission, was working on an updated master plan. His firm's draftsmen did some work for the understaffed Plan Commission without charge to the city. Schwarz managed his interconnections straightforwardly, and there was no hint of gain to the firm. However, in 1961, when the firm, then Russell Mullgardt Schwarz Van Hoefen, was in the early stages of several projects advocated by the plan commission, Schwarz resigned both his office and his membership in the commission to avoid conflicts of interest. He died in 1971.

In 1967 the City of St. Louis and Downtown, Inc., agreed to sponsor a national competition financed by the business group for design of the Gateway Mall, with a $15,000 first prize. The program, written by Charles E. King, chairman of the Chapter's urban design committee, and approved by the American Institute of Architects and the American Society of Landscape Architects, defined the site as from Memorial Drive to Twenty-first Street, but designated the blocks between Memorial Drive and Twelfth Street as the first priority.

The program gave broad latitude to concepts, means, materials, and uses. The Chapter president and vice-president, Angelo G. Corrubia and Nolan L. Stinson, Jr., and Joseph Passonneau were on the competition committee. The judges were Lawrence B. Anderson, head of the School of Architecture and Planning,

Massachusetts Institute of Technology; Harris Armstrong; Thomas D. Church, landscape architect, San Francisco; Charles W. Moore, chairman, Department of Architecture, Yale University; John Simonds, Pittsburgh; and Mayor Alfonso J. Cervantes.

The concept of a linear public space as an expression of the westward axial thrust of the Gateway Arch had been persuasively advocated in an article written for the *Post-Dispatch* by Edmund N. Bacon, the planner who had guided Philadelphia's strategies for new-and-old redevelopment.

Most of the fifty-seven competition entries addressed themselves to active uses of the priority blocks, and several proposed a prominent structure west of the Milles Fountain, built on air rights over the highway ramps there, as a visual terminus. The designs included skating rinks, pedestrian ways under vaulted glass, an aquarium, paved terraces with shops and food, outdoor dining, water features, elevated and sunken gardens—generally festive and some cultural uses of the strip. Architects' Week showcased the entries in an exhibition at the Old Courthouse.

The winning scheme, by Sasaki, Dawson, DeMay Associates of Waterbury, Massachusetts, called for plantings of four rows of trees on berms along each side of a grassy swale, from Broadway to Eleventh Street and from Twelfth to Eighteenth. Pedestrians strolling along the swale would be isolated by the trees and berms from automobile traffic on Market and Chestnut; a two-level parking garage was under the east end.

A jury member said that street traffic, seen as a possible deterrent to pedestrian access, had some bearing on the choice of a passive mall. Murphy & Mackey won second place for an elevated mall between Seventh and Tenth streets, with street-level cultural and commercial activities and a fountain basin between Ninth and Tenth.

The block between Tenth and Eleventh streets was graded and planted as a trial of the winning prescription, and it aroused an outpouring of apathy. The city removed the trees and graded away the berms, which struck some as resembling bunkers. Public and business interests were united in demanding activity in the heart of the city more dynamic than watching grass grow, but that was the last moment of accord. The Gateway Mall was back to Square One, and it became one of the city's most divisive issues.

Efforts to salvage something from the Sasaki plan were abandoned. The city could not qualify for federal funds, and after fifteen stop-and-go years, four privately funded proposals for the blocks between Sixth and Tenth streets made it to the Board of Aldermen in 1982. One by Gateway Mall Redevelopment Corporation (later, Pride Redevelopment Corporation), with HOK and Team Four, called for low buildings along the north sides of the Seventh-to-Eleventh blocks, the south sides landscaped for a half mall.

Another, by Landmark Redevelopment Corporation, with Richard Claybour, called for renovation of the Buder and Title Guaranty buildings, designed by William A. Swasey and Eames & Young, respectively, side-by-side on Seventh Street. Also included was the Eames & Young International Building in the same block (all nominated to the National Register). That plan also called for construction of four office buildings, a hotel, a bank and related amenities.

Mackey & Associates called for the rehabilitation of the Title Guaranty Building. Market Square Redevelopment Corporation, with Sverdrup & Parcel, suggested a one-block parking structure with retail space on the Sixth-to-Seventh block.

An argument for removing the twelve-story Title Guaranty, across Chestnut Street from the ten-story Wainwright, was that the Wainwright would be prominently in view for the first time, a strong visual asset to the mall. Architectural historians contended, however, that a still higher priority was to preserve all the historic buildings in their significant contextual relationship with the Wainwright.

The Tenth-to-Eleventh block had been committed by then for the sculpture *Twain* by Richard Serra.

The Chapter entered this thicket in search of a consensus of professional and public opinion. Clark Davis and Helen DiFate, joint chairs of the public relations committee, organized a public forum at the Old Courthouse on April 29, 1982, to hear a discussion moderated by president Robert G. Galloway. The overflow audience of general public and Chapter members included Mayor Vincent C. Schoemehl, Jr. A then-and-there vote of the Chapter members showed a majority in favor of the ''half-mall''plan. Galloway announced the Chapter's position: 'While we do not necessarily consider any plan to be optimal in every respect at this particular economic time, we believe that the Gateway Mall Redevelopment Corporation's plan represents the best overall direction for mall development.''

The controversy intensified when the city adopted a significantly compromised variation of the favored plan, providing for three new medium-height buildings to

A netfull of balloons is about to be released in celebration of a dark moment in St. Louis's preservation history. The International Building collapses in a cloud of dust and the Buder begins to sag as both were imploded in 1984.

replace existing, similarly scaled historic structures that had previously been characterized as too tall. On the eve of the demolition hearing, the Chapter's historic buildings committee drew up a resolution in support of saving the historic buildings, and asked the executive committee to poll the members. A postcard mailing requesting members to vote by telephone recorded fifty-six percent for the resolution.

At the hearing, March 29, 1983, Gerhardt Kramer reported: "It is the opinion of the committee that the Buder, Title Guaranty, and International buildings are of historic value and that further effort should be made to incorporate them into the design of the Mall." The Title Guaranty was demolished by wrecking ball in April 1983 and the Buder and International were imploded in August 1984 to make way for the Gateway One Building and its half-mall plaza. A series of photographs by Arthur Matia, documenting the twenty seconds of destruction, won a merit award in the Chapter's 1985 Photo Contest.

Chapter presidents voiced members' misgivings as the mall moved steadily toward failure: Thomas M. Tebbetts, regarding clearance of the Tenth-Eleventh block for the Serra sculpture: "... we are not negative to the Serra sculpture per se. ... We are objecting only to the process or lack of it that allows a portion of the mall to be redesigned without a master plan." (*St. Louis Construction News & Review,* March 16, 1977.)

H. Curtis Ittner, in the twentieth anniversary year of the Gateway Arch: "This missed opportunity to keep the mall area an open space should be a warning not to let developer economics destroy critical urban spaces in our city where future generations will be forced to live with our mistakes." (*St. Louis Post-Dispatch,* November 15, 1985.)

At the end of his term, president Clark S. Davis wrote in the *Post-Dispatch* (December 3, 1988) about the partially conceived mall and the Chapter's role in the 1982 controversy: "After decades of planning for the Gateway Mall—and all of the promises of the last few years—the incredible fact is that there is no plan guiding the Mall's proper completion. ... It was exciting to think that St. Louis might finally deal conclusively with one of its most important urban spaces. The idea that one thoughtful and coherent plan might be realized seemed more important, at the time, than the immediate choice among the schemes which were presented. Today, the mall is a collection of ideas which have no real design relationship.

The one commercial office project that has been completed by Pride [Redevelopment Corporation] is very much its own statement, despite its sensitive context. The new plaza on the south half of this block belongs totally to the building itself, and not perceptibly to a larger idea for the half mall that was promised. The building controls the site with granite plinths on the south corners. ...."

He characterized the Morton D. May Amphitheater, designed by Team Four for the Sixth-to-Seventh block after the May Department Stores Company transferred its lease on most of that block to the city, as "a popular people place; its form has been controversial, but it is a relief from the dullness of Kiener Plaza next door. At the other end of the blocks slated for redevelopment, Richard Serra's sculpture *Twain* is viewed by most people as an object on the lawn; it is experienced from within, as intended, by only a few." The Chapter executive committee had declined to endorse the Serra installation. William Albinson, chairman of the Environmental and Urban Design Committee, noted that while the block as landscaped according to the Gateway Mall competition design was an "esthetic and functional failure," to redesign it for the monumental sculpture might be "replacing one unworkable solution with another."

Mayor Schoemehl admitted that the 1982 decision-making process was flawed, and in August 1990, the *Post-Dispatch,* which had praised the "open park space" of the half mall, denounced the obliterative new building, which had somehow gone up to fifteen stories, and its "private plaza," and declared, "Junk the half-mall plan."

Gerhardt Kramer, restorer of historic buildings throughout the St. Louis region and consultant for many others, examines a baluster of the Martin Franklin Hanley House, Clayton, in preparation for one of the first Architects' Sunday tours. Kramer served as guide on most of the Chapter-sponsored tours of historic properties.

14
Architects' Sunday:
Taking the Show on the Road

In THE LATE SIXTIES and the seventies, the Chapter broadened its community services, which some members found more challenging than the routine of regular monthly meetings. It enlarged student programs, greatly aided by a scholarship bequest, and it extended the public's experience with building and design—bringing architecture to the public in exhibitions and taking the public to three-dimensional architecture in tours that became monthly outings, some more ambitious than had been tried before.

Chapter members were active on national and regional levels. George E. Kassabaum was installed as president of the Institute at its 1968 convention in Portland, Oregon, at which George McCue, an honorary member, was awarded the first national AIA Architecture Critic's Citation. The May 1969 MARA convention and its associated Architects' Week celebrated Kassabaum's election with a testimonial dinner-dance, and in the next year Rex Becker became national treasurer. Robert Elkington was in charge

of the 1968 Regional Central States Convention, focused on recreational architecture and held at Tan-Tar-A, on the Lake of the Ozarks.

During Nolan Stinson's presidency in 1968 and 1969, the Chapter developed community assistance programs and increased efforts to direct students and young architects toward the AIA. Kenneth Schaefer, the 1970 president, and his wife, Miriam, furthered this activity with monthly beer and pretzel meetings with students at their home. In 1970 the Chapter cooperated with the Citizen Volunteer Corps by giving free architectural advice (but no drawings) to needy persons and businesses. In lieu of a 1971 summer party, it held a clean-up day to paint Pavilion 16 near the south entrance of Tower Grove Park. In conjunction with the Community Design Workshop in 1972, members designed and painted supergraphics at Kinder Cottage, Inc., a pre-school facility at Union Methodist Church.

The program that has the most strongly

George E. Kassabaum and his wife, Marjory, with Robert L. Durham, whom Kassabaum succeeded as president of the Institute at the 1968 convention in Portland, Oregon.

stirred and maintained public interest in architects and architecture was, and is, Architects' Sunday, originated by Betty Lou Custer in 1969 and running steadily ever since. Thousands of people have taken advantage of the tours, on the second Sunday of each month, to visit architecturally significant buildings and sites, new and old.

The first tour, in December 1970, was guided by Harris Armstrong through his new Ethical Society Meeting House. Other tours that year included the University City Public Library by Smith & Entzeroth, Lindbergh High School by Charles W. Lorenz and Jack Sorkin, and the 1867 Christ Church Cathedral by Leopold Eidlitz, as renovated in 1969 by Burks & Landberg, with its 1963 chapel renovation by Dunn & Stinson. Attendance topped 1,000 persons at some, such as a bus tour of Florissant and a visit to the Daniel Bissell House, restored by Kramer & Harms.

Chapter members prepared maps, fact sheets, signs, and plaques, and helped to guide hundreds of visitors through tour sites within a few hours. Throughout the 1970s and early 1980s, Gerhardt Kramer, generous with his time and knowledge, was the usual leader of bus tours to outlying places, some with overnight stops; these were often preceded by background slide lectures. An early bus group toured Bernard Maybeck's Principia College campus and buildings at Elsah, Illinois, and modern buildings on the campus by Kenneth E. Wischmeyer & Partners and Smith & Entzeroth.

Architects' Sunday brought acclaim to the Chapter. Custer was invited to write about it for the May 1971 *AIA Journal,* and to report its success in public outreach on an AIA convention panel in 1972. The Atlanta Chapter, among others, instituted similar programs. Following Kramer, Karl Pettit assisted with Architects' Sunday, and in 1990-91 Carolyn Toft, executive director of Landmarks Association of St. Louis, Inc., and an honorary member of the Institute, jointly administered the program.

The Missouri Association of Registered Architects had no formal affiliation with the AIA, and in 1970 it was replaced with the Missouri Council of Architects, designed to function as the AIA's state organization. MCA directors elected by the Chapter represented its interests before the legislature, and Chapter members automatically became MCA members, with the Chapter collecting and paying annual dues. However, the Chapter opposed an Octagon effort, in 1974, to further strengthen the MCA with a liaison role. The Kansas City and St. Louis chapters joined in insisting on direct rela-

The celebration of George Kassabaum's inauguration as Institute President took place at a Central States Region reception at the Portland Hilton Hotel. Standing: George Hellmuth, W. Allen Cleneay, Rex Becker, George McCue, Nolan Stinson, George Kassabaum, Chester Roemer, Edward Bartz, Angelo Corrubia, H. Curtis Itt-ner, Baker Word, Jean Schneeberger, and Ralph Fournier. Seated: Kathryn Stinson, Laurine Cleneay, Mimi Hellmuth, Ada Becker, Marjory Kassabaum, Bernice Roemer, Margaret Corrubia, Marilyn Bartz, and Mary Jane Fournier.

tionships with the Institute.

Meanwhile, the Chapter was occupied with internal managerial and housekeeping details. Jean Schneeberger, who had served part-time as executive secretary since 1957, was made full-time in 1965, with part-time assistance by Margaret Poelker. Ann Walsh became executive secretary in 1969, and Poelker was made full-time to manage documents and forms

services, for which, in 1971, the Chapter acquired exclusive distributor rights.

Under Kenneth Schaefer, this profitable, high-demand enterprise was set up as a division. Despite limited shelf space, it was expanded into the bookstore operation, with specialized works for professionals and titles of general architectural interest to the drop-in public. With Walsh's resignation in April 1972, Betty

Past presidents of the Women's Architectural League celebrated its tenth anniversary with a luncheon at the Bath and Tennis Club in 1970. Louise (Mrs. Harris) Armstrong, the first president, is at left; others are Bee (Mrs. Donald) Freeman, Micki (Mrs. Eric) Smith, Bernice (Mrs. Chester) Roemer, Norma (Mrs. William)

Rupe, Kathryn (Mrs. Nolan) Stinson, Doris (Mrs. Charles) Danna, Minne (Mrs. John A.) Grunik, Patricia (Mrs. Bryce) Hastings, the current president; and Harriet (Mrs. Merlin E.) Lickhalter. Ada (Mrs. Rex) Becker, was not present.

Architects' Sunday at the Daniel Bissell House, 1970: Kayo Stinson, Nancy (Mrs. Richard) Bliss, Ravenna and Gerhardt Kramer, Emily Bliss, and Kay (Mrs.

Walter B.) Kromm. Kramer & Harms were the restoration architects.

In 1971, Chapter volunteers painted an 1871 gazebo in Tower Grove Park, as documented in *this drawing by Joseph D. Murphy of the crew at work.*

Lou Custer was made executive secretary and, replacing a part-time consultant, director of public relations—principally for Architects' Sunday. In the same year, Custer became the fourteenth woman to be elected to the College of Fellows and the only one in the Chapter's history.

The explosion of an old ammonia air-conditioning system in the basement of the Wainwright Building blew out store-front windows, caused other non-structural damage, and sent the Chapter on a hunt for new quarters. The owners, who had kept the building alive through a long period of low-occupancy and stalled preservation activity, announced an intention to use the insurance money to replace the building with a parking lot.

Like others concerned with the fate of the Wainwright, the Chapter had encouraged the owners to undertake rehabilitation. In 1967, it developed restoration guidelines written by W. Philip Cotton, Jr., and Theodore J. Wofford, and in 1971 it published a brochure, written by Cotton, on the building's architectural significance.

Following the explosion, the Chapter and Landmarks Association joined in a task-force study headed by Chester Roemer for a seventy-five-page report, "Recommendations for Restoration of the Wainwright Building." Its main thrust was toward economical modernization within the historic shell, and it helped to persuade Missouri Governor Christopher Bond to favor adapting the Wainwright for state offices. Richard Bliss, Cotton, and Wofford participated in this study, for which Roemer received a Chapter citation. The Chapter moved out in 1974.

With the National Trust for Historic Preservation in close touch, the Institute and the state jointly administered a two-phase competition for the Wainwright state office complex, which included remodeling and restoration, and an additional 115,000 gross square feet of office space to be built on the rest of the block. Two St. Louis firms placed: William B. Ittner with the Chicago and New York offices of Perkins & Will; and the winning team of Hastings & Chivetta with the Philadelphia and New York offices of Mitchell/Giurgola. The seven-man jury included Hugh Hardy, Gunnar Birkerts, and historian Vincent Scully. The completed project was dedicated June 5, 1981.

Chapter members, pleased with the easy access and public exposure of downtown ground-floor space, applauded a location chosen in the Paul Brown Building. But on the morning of signing a lease, a space in the Syndicate Trust Building that had been priced beyond the Chapter's means suddenly was offered on more favorable terms, and was eagerly accepted. It had the advantages of both street and lobby access and exposure. Robert Holland, of Wedemeyer Cernik Corrubia, designed the new office to include a display window and shelving for the expanding bookstore. Thomas M. Tebbetts, of Wischmeyer Architects, produced the working drawings, and forty-nine member firms contributed $6,550 toward relocation expenses.

When the Chapter moved in August 1974, Betty Lou Custer's position was upgraded from executive secretary to executive director; Margaret Poelker was made director of publications and membership services. The Olive Street office, the Chapter's home for thirteen years, provided a highly visible presence on one of the busiest pedestrian streets. By 1976 the flourishing bookstore was stocking 750 titles and listing more than 2,000 selections. Kenneth Schaefer was elected to the College of Fellows for service to the AIA in this and other projects.

The Chapter had established itself in the public arena as a source of stimulating ideas in the early 1970s, a time of social and political cross-purposes. Besides Architects' Sunday and the Speakers' Bureau, its activities included a two-year series of monthly travel programs, "Armchair Tours Through the Architect's Eyes," coordinated by Custer and Chester Roemer, at the University City Public Library (1972-74). In conjunction with a 1972 Institute promotion, "WHY accept ugliness—WHY NOT beautify the environment?" the Chapter initiated monthly newspaper articles about city places in need of design attention, and asked twelve member firms to propose remedial possibilities.

Murphy, Downey, Wofford & Richman took aim at the troublesome Gateway Mall with an elaboration of the Murphy & Mackey competition scheme—a pedestrian park elevated over cross-streets from the Gateway Arch to Union Station; the upper level with all-season attractions such as a plaza with band pavilion and carillon tower, demountable cages for animal shows, kiosks, a reflecting pool/skating rink, and street-level theaters, art galleries, and restaurants.

Schemes for other sites included an HOK proposal for mixed-use development in the Mill Creek Valley between Seventh and Tenth streets; one by Smith & Ent-

Delegates to San Francisco convention, 1973— Stand- ing: Rex Becker, Donald Porter Wilson, Charles Danna, Merlin Lickhalter, William Rupe, Joseph D. Murphy, *Baker Word, J. Robert Green, Betty Lou Custer. Seated: Bryce Hastings, D. Robert Downey, Joseph Cernik, and Chester Roemer.*

zeroth for landscaping to define the Clayton Road entry to the DeMun Neighborhood; and a pedestrian plaza around the North Grand Water Tower by Laurent J. Torno, Jr., of Berger, Field, Torno, Hurley. All were exhibited at the Central States Conference in Wichita in 1973.

Architecture was immediately depressed by the energy crisis and material shortages of 1974, and it remained in recession for several years. "Certainly there will be new challenges for all segments of the profes-

sion and the construction industry," president Joseph Cernik wrote in the January 1974 *Newsletter.*

The Chapter promoted a uniform building code for the entire metropolitan area as a way to expedite construction and cut costs. Construction-related lawsuits and escalating professional liability insurance were adding to overhead to a degree that the AIA viewed as out of control, and the Chapter endorsed a revised statute of limitations bill.

15
Expanding Services and the Ranft Fund

As PRACTICE BECAME more complex and competitive, the Institute intensified attention to continuing education for its own members. Chapter seminars and workshops were focused on topics relating to professional survival—office management, the recession, marketing strategies, fees, legal protection. ". . . Architects must explore new areas [in which] to provide services or shrink significantly in size and stature in the coming years," said president Tebbetts in 1977. Architects were encouraged to move in the direction of comprehensive services, such as life-cycle costing studies, energy use and conservation studies, cost estimating, environmental impact statements, historic preservation, construction management, interior design—even design-build, previously deplored as unprofessional and unethical.

Tebbetts made energy-efficient design the focus of his administration, building on a study by an eighteen-member task force. Chapter programs and seminars delved into solar collector systems, building orientation, insulation, infiltration prevention, new insulating and reflecting glasses, and thermal-break windows. The *Newsletter* carried a column by Charles B. Hook, chairman of the education committee, listing nation-wide seminars and workshops in those areas. The Chapter bookstore stocked publications about energy-efficient design. The public was invited to pick up a Solar Energy Reference Roster at the office; it listed architectural firms qualified to offer counsel on natural-resource (solar and wind) energy.

Back from the 1978 national convention, president Charles Danna spoke of the need for architecture to reexamine its traditional positions and to enlarge its services. "We can blame it on the new wave of consumerism, the economy of our times with its raw competitive by-product and/or the rising societal expectations of accountability," Danna said. "The membership voted to consider design-build and contracting by architects on an experimental three-year basis [and] moderate liberalization of the present advertising rules to meet the constitutional Bates and O'Steen case guidelines, allowing members to purchase advertising in newspapers, periodicals, directories, or other publications."

In the past, the most innocuous advertising by an architect had been cause for his rejection for Chapter membership. Danna noted that the convention had been more "minority-minded" than in the past. "I think AIA architects are showing more maturity in their social and professional responsibilities."

Other aspects of the profession were changing so rapidly that chapters in several states endorsed continuing education as a requirement for membership. The St. Louis Chapter supported voluntary continuing education by offering, jointly with the Producers' Council, monthly workshops on architectural and construction topics, open to AIA members and persons in the building industries. Formed under Danna's presidency, those programs have been directed since then by Louis Malin, Jon R. Pantaleoni, Thomas H. Saunders, and by Randall Miltenberger, who has continued as chairman since 1983.

On a memorable day in 1978, H. Curtis Ittner received a call from the Boatmen's Trust Company advising him that the St. Louis AIA Scholarship Fund had inherited $530,000 from the Hester Ranft and Ruth Ranft trusts. Ittner had been a trustee of the scholarship fund since 1971, when it was worth about $35,000, and chairman since 1973. The principal benefactor was Ralph P. Ranft, a Chapter member who practiced in St. Louis for more than forty years before his death in 1965. Hester Ranft was his widow. Ruth Ranft, their daughter, remained close to the Chapter through the WAL and friends after his death. Hester died in 1976 and Ruth in 1978. They bequeathed the majority of their estate to what was to be called the Ralph Ranft Scholarship Fund.

Since the bequest, the fund has grown to more than $1 million, and has provided $450,000 in loans and grants to students, as well as support for student and professional design charrettes, the Architectural Awareness in Schools Program initiated by the Chapter in the 1980s, and memorial lectures by distinguished architects. The latter, in Steinberg Auditorium, Washington University, contribute to the Monday night lecture series of the School of Architecture. Other aid to students is offered by the Kassabaum and Masonry Institute scholarships which, with the Ranft Fund, are administered under the umbrella of the original St. Louis Chapter AIA Scholarship Fund.

In another approach to strengthening its bonds with students and young architects, the Chapter inaugurated Architects' Saturday under president William W. Rupe in 1976, as an introduction to the intricacies of architectural practice. The public was also invited. Each month, a firm would open its office on a Saturday afternoon, with staff on hand to discuss its work and procedures. One of the first visitations was to Rupe's own office, Anselevicius/Rupe Associates, at 379 North Big Bend, near the Washington University campus. Rupe's partner, George Anselevicius, had been dean of the School of Architecture from 1967 until 1973, when he became dean of Harvard's Graduate School of Design. On a 1978 field trip, with Charles Danna as president, the Chapter hosted thirty students for a bus tour of architectural offices and lunch at the Daniel Bissell House.

Both Anselevicius and his successor as dean, Constantine Michaelides, were active in the Chapter, which maintained close and cordial relations with the School of Architecture. Several Chapter members began teaching in the school's Architectural Technology Program, which offered a Certificate in Architectural Technology and a Bachelor of Technology.

One of the Chapter's most ambitious and effective community projects was the 1976 report on the conservation of Forest Park prepared by the AIA Regional/Urban Design Assistance Team (R/UDAT). Eugene Mackey III chaired the committee that assembled urban and land-use specialists to evaluate the park from a national perspective. Provocative questions were put to the group: How important is Forest Park to St. Louis? How much change can and should it absorb? What is its full potential for serving St. Louis? The extensively publicized report was instrumental in the founding of Forest Park Forever, a citizens' committee to oversee park development and restoration, and it continues to serve as a resource for long-range planning. William Albinson, Richard Claybour, and president Rupe assisted Mackey in this effort.

To fund R/UDAT, the St. Louis Chapter AIA Foundation was established to receive tax-deductible contributions. In 1990, under Mackey's leadership, the foundation was reorganized as the St. Louis Foundation for Architecture, based on a similar institution in Boston, to advance its potential for becoming one of the Chapter's most significant agencies in its second century.

Super Sunday, a 1978 architectural fair set up in Kiener Plaza, featured crafts and art exhibits, informational booths, and a "Solar Van," with AIA balloons and T-shirts to emphasize it as an architectural occasion. It was organized by Charles and Doris Danna in conjunction with an Architects' Sunday tour of the HOK Boatmen's Tower, 100 North Broadway, in which the architect's offices and the law offices of Husch, Eppenberger, Donohue, Elson & Cornfeld, by Burks Associates, were open to visitors. The impact of Super Sunday was prolonged with illustrated lunch-hour talks on the city's architectural heritage in the downtown Famous-Barr auditorium by Richard Bliss, Gerhardt Kramer, John Schulte, Edward Bartz, and president Charles Danna, who concluded the series with a presentation, "Where Do We Go From Here?"

Having developed skill, confidence, and a track record in civic affairs, the Chapter increasingly made itself heard on issues affecting the city's urban character. Its involvement in Forest Park planning gave it a firm basis for publishing a resolution opposing expansion of Children's Hospital on air rights over Kingshighway (to the edge of the park) as "an irrevocable action which produces an expedient solution to what should be a long-range question."

Historic preservation and adaptive reuse of architecturally significant buildings became major concerns. In 1978, president Charles Danna was outspoken regarding preservation of Union Station, "which is, along with the Wainwright Building, the most significant piece of architecture in St. Louis." He sponsored a unanimously adopted Chapter resolution for relocating the National Museum of Transport to the station trainshed.

Laclede's Landing, entered on the National Register of Historic Places in 1976, was emerging as a showcase for creative reuse of old warehouse buildings, of which several were chosen for Architects' Sunday tours. One tour featured the Old Judge Coffee Building, 1884, by Alfred Grable and Auguste Weber, and converted by The Hoffmann Partnership for its offices and tenants. Raeder Place, 1872, designed by Frederick Raeder and renovated by Kimble A. Cohn & Associates, was another attraction. A third was the Witte Hardware Building, 1905, by Ernst C. Janssen and renovated by HOK. With an Institute grant of $2,000 in 1975, William Albinson and Peter H. Green produced a seventeen-minute film, "Re/Vision," on the recycling of old urban buildings.

The emergence of post-modern design in the late 1970s stirred the interest of students and professionals. Some of its leading practitioners were brought to Washington University in the fall of 1978 for a two-day conference, "Directions," organized by students and partly funded by the Chapter. Visiting speakers Peter Eisenman, Michael Graves, Stanley Tigerman, Robert Stern, and Nory Miller took part with faculty members William Gass, Udo Kultermann, and Norris Kelly Smith.

The Chapter's next outreach to School of Architecture students, in the following year, was sponsorship of an exhibition organized by Randall Miltenberger, "Celebration of Architecture," in the Steinberg Hall main gallery. It put projects by twenty-three member firms on view, with a representative of each firm meeting with students one afternoon during the display.

16

Women in the AIA, Student Outreach, the Charrettes

B
Y 1980, THE AMERICAN Institute of
Architects and its chapters could take
pride in impressive membership gains—
with interesting side effects. The majority
of members now worked for large firms,
while the majority of firms were small
practices, and this paradox confronted the
AIA with an extended gamut of needs for
member services. The proportions of
membership available for public service
also grew larger, and the Chapter could
draw upon fresh energies for classroom
programs and for innovative urban design
studies such as the annual Charrette.

In St. Louis, the membership range was
from offices whose entire staff could fit into a compact car up to the gigantic HOK
and Sverdrup organizations with hundreds
of employees, including interior and
graphic designers, planners, landscape architects, and engineers at bases in this
country and abroad. The largest and the
smallest firms, and the many in between,
had quite different needs and interests.
Moreover, the membership included increasing numbers of women and ethnic
minorities. The accompanying shifts of

emphasis—social, legal, economic, and
programmatic—made the old legacy of the
intimate club remote and meaningless.

Expanding services and programs put
increasing strains on resources of Institute
and Chapter. The obvious solutions were
to build membership still more and increase dues, and both strategies were
called into play. Membership categories
were restructured in 1977 to expand Institute rosters. Previously, Chapter
members who were newly registered architects were not automatically admitted to
the Institute but were held in a three-year
local membership category called Professional Associate, and then had to apply to
become a Corporate Member of the Institute with the right to use ''AIA'' after
the name). The other categories were:
Associate (unlicensed architects or
technical personnel), Associate of AIA
(unlicensed persons in related professions
or, if licensed, only if they had been such
for no more than three years), Professional
Affiliate, and Student Associate.

Under the new rules, all registered architects who are Chapter members must

also become members of the Institute, and the local Professional Associate category is dropped. Four classifications now exist: Member (licensed architects in architectural firms), Associate (unlicensed architects and technical personnel employed by architectural firms), Professional Affiliate (persons in allied disciplines), and Student Affiliate. An Emeritus status for retired members is conferred upon request.

In 1980 Thomas Teasdale, a newly enrolled Fellow and vice-president of the Institute, reported to the Chapter that national membership had increased by thirty percent in the previous three years, but that the Institute could not sustain an equivalent growth rate in the already expanded member services. How to allocate limited resources to the satisfaction of a highly diversified membership was, he said, "one of the greatest internal challenges facing the AIA."

The Chapter had periodically launched aggressive membership drives since the 1960s, when Betty Lou Custer headed that activity, with growth to 525 members by 1980, an increase of 175 members in ten years. In 1977 when the membership was at 427, approximately 200 eligible nonmembers were practicing in the St. Louis area. All were contacted, but membership increases alone could not fully solve the Chapter's budget problems. Sales of books and documents, which had accounted for up to forty-six percent of the Chapter's income, had declined by 1980, causing a significant deficit. Since the 1973 dues increase, expenditures had risen 123 percent, and the executive committee decided that another increase was necessary. In 1983 the membership approved a fifteen-dollar increase, raising an-

nual dues to $120. It squeaked through on the second ballot.

Despite the increasing presence of women in the American work force, few of them chose architecture until the 1980s, when the previous trickle of women entering the profession grew to numbers substantial enough to make their presence felt. In recognition of this, the Chapter took the action customary for engagement with unfamiliar phenomena—it organized a task force. It was formed in 1984, was named Women in Architecture (WIA), and was headed by Susan Behrens. One objective was to examine how the Chapter might encourage more women to join the AIA and become active in its programs. A 1973 Institute survey found that only 1.2 percent of registered architects were women, and that women represented only 3.7 percent of the "architectural population."

By 1980, women in the Chapter had advanced a small step to 3.6 percent of the membership (nineteen of 525). Behrens developed the task force into a standing committee open to all women architects and interns in the metropolitan area. By 1986 the WIA had a directory listing 120 women, including twenty-three AIA members and eighteen associates. The WIA sponsors Chapter programs and originates others of its own. It organizes fellowship gatherings and tours of architectural projects in which its members are involved, and it looks for leadership opportunities for women within the AIA. It maintains a slide archive of its members' projects. By 1990 the Chapter roster of 690 members included forty-two women—six percent, and close to the national average of 8.4 percent.

Female students now (1991) make up

Chapter delegates to the 1979 national convention in Kansas City. Back row: Barry Evens, Robert Dethloff, Milton J. Bischof, Jr., David Pearce, Edward W. Wilhelms, Frank J. Gruchalla, Jr., James T. Biehle, Gerhardt Kramer, Gale Hill, and Kenneth Schaefer. Middle row: Betty Lou Custer, Jane Piper, Doris Dan-na, Susan Danna, Susan Galloway, J. Robert Green, Nelson Schneeberger, Scot Rogers, and Mary Jane Fournier. Front row: William Albinson, Robert Galloway, Charles Danna, Thomas Teasdale, Laurance P. Berri, William Pistrui, Anthony DeMichele, Eugene J. Mackey III.

31.9 percent of the undergraduate enrollment in the Washington University School of Architecture and forty-two percent of the graduate students—auguring an increased female representation in the profession. Following Behrens as chair were Roberta Lawrence, Marion Bess Smith, Sara Harrison, and Jane Godfrey.

The great turning point of recognition of women in architecture is, of course, the fact that in 1993 the president of the American Institute of Architects will be Susan A. Maxman, of Philadelphia. The Chapter's turning point comes a year sooner—its president-elect for 1992 is Doris Danna.

Women of both Chapter and WAL have become increasingly active in the educational programs. Well-working professional rapport with college and high school students encouraged the Chapter into programs addressed to primary and secondary schools, public and private. The concept was to use the classroom as a laboratory for learning about the built environment by enlisting architects, teachers, and students in the design and construction of projects such as play structures, art display units, and puppet theaters.

The program, Architectural Awareness in Schools (AAIS), was formulated in 1979 by a task force headed by Harry Richman. Susan Galloway, wife of Robert Galloway and a professional teacher,

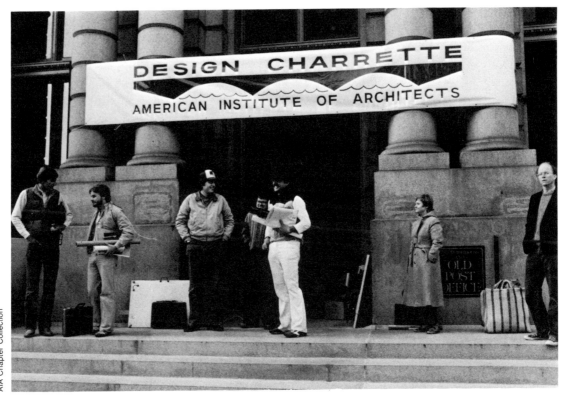

The time, 7 A.M.; the place, steps of the Old Post Office; the people, young architects waiting to begin work on the first Charrette, 1982. The project, development of a park on the East Side levee.

served as coordinator with educators, and a pilot program was scheduled for the 1980-81 school year. Edward Wilhelms chaired the AAIS committee, and Janet Rothberg White, a Chapter member, was employed as program director. Funding came from a Missouri Arts Council grant to the Educational Confederation, the St. Louis AIA Scholarship Fund, participating schools and districts, the WAL and AIA members, friends, and firms. This program would continue for five years, with forty-nine projects designed and constructed in thirty-four schools.

The Awareness program included teacher-training workshops, and in 1985 Susan Galloway began offering a summer graduate-level course at the University of Missouri, St. Louis, for teachers with participation by Richard Bliss and Karl Pettit. Support for this program came from MCA, the Kansas City Chapter AIA, and the St. Louis AIA Scholarship Fund. William M. Pistrui, the 1980 Chapter president, recalled a decade later that the AAIS program "had a significant impact on developing a public sensitivity to the built environment through direct contact with teachers and students in our educational system."

The annual AIA Charrette, begun in 1982 at the suggestion of Doris Danna, became a prominent public activity. The first Charrette (a Beaux-Arts term for the handcart in which plans were gathered for judging, and by extension the study exercise itself) addressed the shabby spectacle of the Mississippi River bank directly across from the Gateway Arch. A task force headed by Doris Danna wrote a program proposing its development as a permanent park for the annual Veiled Prophet Fair and for the 2004 World's Fair or Summer Olympics, with rapid-transit linkage to St. Louis—first stage of an area-wide light rail system.

Architects and students were invited to gather for a thirty-six-hour charrette on how this might take physical form, with multiple solutions to be presented to the public. Nationally recognized architects—Stuart Cohen, Jorge Silvetti, Gerhardt Kallman, and planner David Lewis—were invited to comment on the projects at a public forum the next day, and entries and critiques were compiled for publication to reach a broader audience.

The success of that program made the Charrette an annual event, managed by a standing committee. Subsequent charrettes have studied the Hyde Park neighborhood (1983), linkage between the central business district and the Jefferson National Expansion Memorial (1984), the Grand Center district (1985), Chouteau's Landing (1986), a central transportation transfer point in Mill Creek Valley (1987), the waterways of Forest Park (1988), and the Delmar Station of the future light rail system (1990). (A charrette was not held in 1989.) Doris Danna's connection with the charrettes, reduced to a less gruelling twelve-hour program, has continued, with Albert B. Fuller, Jr., John R. Reeve, and Bryan E. Sechrist as chairmen. Prestigious architects and critics who have served as judges include Charles Moore, Paul Rudolf, Rodolfo Machado, and Robert Campbell. Whenever possible, one of the judges remains an extra day to deliver the Ralph Ranft Memorial Lecture.

The charrettes furthered Chapter-university relationships by involving students in program planning and in actual design work by faculty-student teams not only from Washington University but also from Kansas State University, the University of Kansas, the University of Illinois, and the St. Louis Community College at Meramec. The mayor of St. Louis, aldermen, other community leaders, and the press are invited to each public forum, and participate in open discussion. Charrette solutions to some problems, notably the East St. Louis riverfront, Grand Center, Jefferson Memorial linkage, and Forest Park waterways have stimulated progress toward concrete planning.

The Intern Development Program (IDP) was launched in 1983, in conjunction with the National Council of Architectural Registration Boards, to provide a structured professional development plan for preparing recent graduates for the registration examination and offering practical training. Joseph Cernik chaired its coordination committee, and get-acquainted workshops were held in 1984 and 1985 for firm principals and IDP candidates. Up to forty firms have taken part. Its successes have been to underscore the responsibility of member firms for advancing the training of young architects and to provide a framework within which recent graduates, including women, could gain exposure and respect as professionals.

Intern architects were taken another step into Chapter relationships in 1985,

Having been presented with a T-shirt emblazoned with the logo of the 1984 charrette, "The Riverfront Connection," Mayor Vincent C. Schoemehl, Jr., displays it for the committee.

Chapter President Gregory Palermo is seated at left, Albert B. Fuller, Jr., right. Standing: John R. Reeve, Doris Danna, Lawrence M. Malcic.

when the group elected an associate director to serve a one-year term with the Chapter board with full voting privileges. Warren Feldman, associate director in 1987, instituted the *Associates Newsletter,* and profiles of interns were featured in the Chapter *Newsletter.*

In 1982, George Edward Kassabaum, a founding principal of Hellmuth, Obata & Kassabaum and past president of the Institute and of the St. Louis Chapter, died

of a stroke at the age of sixty-one. After graduation from the Washington University School of Architecture in 1947, Kassabaum served on the faculty for three years, and former students were among those who looked to him as a mentor. His son, Douglas G. Kassabaum, is a member of the St. Louis Chapter. George Kassabaum was made a Fellow in 1967 for service to the profession.

17
The Chapter Militant

IN THE PUBLIC ARENA, the Chapter learned that although its positions were concentrated on issues of architecture and design, they might be susceptible to political interpretation. Such was the case with the 1907 Pierce Building, designed by F. C. Bonsack. With an addition to be built to the east, the Pierce would be transformed into an $80 million, 900-room Adam's Mark Hotel, designed and to be built by HBE Corporation. It occurred in Albert Fuller's 1983 term as Chapter president.

The prominent site at Fourth and Chestnut overlooked the Jefferson National Expansion Memorial and Luther Ely Smith Park. The developer's announced intention was a first-class flagship hotel, but the published rendering displayed treatment of the former office facade that fell short of graceful transformation, and cursory design of the new element facing the Gateway Arch.

On behalf of the executive committee, Gregory Palermo drafted a critique that reverberated through the business and design communities: "The banal building proposed is inappropriate to this significant location, lacks the qualities necessary for a memorable flagship hotel, and that it should be heralded as a world class hotel, a gate to St. Louis, is an affront to the aspirations of the citizens of this City. For the City and HBE's investors to accept and fund this insipid box with a hotel label on it as a gateway to St. Louis is a travesty. We urge HBE, its investors, and the City of St. Louis to aim higher for the solution to this opportunity. The next generation expects no less of any of us.''

Betty Lou Custer, who kept count of the Chapter's official utterances, noted that this was its first time to go public with adverse comment about a forthcoming private project. Some members felt that the Chapter should have been polled prior to the statement, but even its critics agreed that the renovation as proposed was ungainly. The issue made headlines, and HBE made modifications that improved the public presentation of the Adam's Mark.

One criticism of the Chapter's action, not related to the design issue but with teeth, charged that the AIA was out of place in attacking the design of a colleague. The HBE Corporation was a design/build firm, one of the so-called "package builders" that had traditionally been viewed by the AIA as a threat to the profession. Even though design/build practice was no longer officially deemed an unethical practice for architects, the criticism of the HBE design recalled the superior tone of a just-distant past. A critical letter to the executive committee picked up on that theme, charging that the Adam's Mark statement "serves to consolidate the image of the Architect as a backbiting, clubby, bitching effete whose ivory-towered monuments' roofs leak." Numerous other letters, however, supported the Chapter's action.

There was more to come. In 1985 the HBE Corporation displayed a model of a block-wide landscaped pedestrian passage over the twelve lanes of Interstate 70 and Memorial Drive between the Gateway Arch grounds and federally-owned Luther Ely Smith Park. The scheme included a garage beneath the park for about 700 cars, which the Adam's Mark said it needed to supplement its internal parking for 300 cars. The proposal was shown to city officials and community leaders before being made public, and was receiving favorable reactions.

The Charrette of the previous October had indicated such a linkage as desirable and the most feasible. However, president Ittner raised questions of traffic congestion not addressed by the garage proposal, as did an executive board statement about the design, read by president-elect Miltenberger at the annual meeting of the Jefferson National Expansion Memorial Association. It commended HBE for

reviving the overpass concept, but as to the garage pointed to ambiguities in "the extent to which the general public will be served as opposed to its use for private hotel purposes."

In an article for the *St. Louis Business Journal* (July 29-August 4, 1985) Eugene Mackey III, chairman of the Chapter's urban design committee, addressed the broader issues of planning goals versus happenstance development: "A developer's proposals are focused on his own economic advantage, and if his self-interest happens to correspond with hastily identified community priorities then we have city planning by lucky coincidence. But if we have no available standards of highest and best uses and design, then we are being motivated entirely in reaction to whatever is presented. In that case, it is the developers who are in charge of St. Louis city planning, and we have planning by default." The problems were left unresolved, and the proposal was dropped.

Meanwhile, the Chapter's more routine committee and staff activities hummed along to increasingly intricate rhythms. Betty Lou Custer had been promoted to executive vice-president, and a succession of assistants included JoAnn Pennington, Jane Piper, Susan Danna, and Mary Wolfe. Programs proliferating over decades did not run themselves. Each new president had to appoint administrators for school and professional workshops, student and craftsmanship awards, charrettes, Architects' Sunday and other tours, a Boy Scout Explorer Post, the AIA Foundation, the Scholarship Fund, and the Steedman Fellowship.

Standing committees dealt with practice, exhibits, government affairs, historic buildings, interior architecture, building codes, Chapter finances, energy conservation, ethics, the exam refresher course, membership, public relations, the speakers' bureau, urban design, and publications. Special programs brought outstanding speakers to address the chapter, including James Marston Fitch, E. Fay Jones, Gunnar Birkerts, John Burgee, and Ulrich Franzen.

As programs accrued, Chapter presidents worked to improve efficiency and communications within these networks. In 1979 President Laurance P. Berri began the practice of putting the vice-president/president-elect in charge of a long-range planning committee. In 1981 President Anthony M. DeMichele reduced the number of standing committees and increased the number of task forces to streamline the committee structure. And in 1988 President Clark S. Davis reorganized the commissioner/committee structure as four commissions, each with four or more committees reporting to it.

Like several of his peers, Davis had gained organizational skills in the larger corporate architectural firms in St. Louis, so occasionally the Chapter would take on a more corporate cast, as in his structuring of reporting hierarchies in bubble-diagram charts. Throughout the change cycles, Betty Lou Custer's firm but sensitive guidance maintained the quality and continuity that made the St. Louis AIA into one of the country's premier chapters.

The Chapter has maintained active relationships with a number of professional and industry-related groups—PRIDE, the American Society of Landscape Architects, American Institute of Planning, Institute of Business Designers, Construction Engineers Council of Missouri, and the Construction Products Council (renamed from the Producers Council).

Following internal improvements, the planning committee of 1983 under Gregory Palermo and the Chapter under his presidency in 1984, concentrated on public issues. He suggested that, given a new readiness by the public in St. Louis and elsewhere to become better informed about architecture and planning, community decision-makers needed to be "targeted with informed perspectives on good design," and that the Chapter should regularly submit position letters to the press on controversial issues.

The statements on the Gateway Mall and Adam's Mark having established the Chapter as a source to be heeded, it made further pronouncements on public issues specifically related to planning and design. It endorsed regional light-rail transit under study in 1983 by the East-West Gateway Coordinating Council, and implementation of a Forest Park master plan (with recommendations for changes before passage); it opposed a domestic animal demonstration farm in Forest Park and a mandated employment quota law covering residency, minorities, and women employees. The Chapter was critical of the appointment of a Heritage and Urban Design commissioner with no background in architecture, history, or urban design, and as a general principle, advocated professional leadership in public offices.

Palermo's successor, H. Curtis Ittner, carried this initiative into his term, noting that "[Mayor Vincent] Schoemehl subsequently sought our advice on urban design issues and placed Chapter members on committees where our opinions are important. [County Supervisor Gene] McNary, who was suspicious of our intentions, did not act on our offer."

Gerhardt Kramer receives the Chapter's Gold Honor Award, 1987, for extraordinary career achievement in historic restoration and as Architects' Sunday guide. His wife, Ravenna, *shares the honor conferred by Chapter President Thomas H. Teasdale, left. Ted Pappas, national AIA president-elect, brought the Institute's congratulations.*

The photo contest, originated by President Albert Fuller in 1983, began as a local competition of slides on architectural subjects, and in two years became the National AIA Architectural Photography Competition with joint sponsorship by the Chapter continuing. In the first year, eight participants entered thirty-six photos, and the jurors, Robert Pettus, Wayne Arteaga, and Eldon Arteaga, gave the first award to Jim Biehle's photograph of the Transamerica Building, San Francisco.

Since 1985 the competition has been open to all AIA members for substantial cash prizes, publication in *Architecture* magazine, and inclusion in an exhibition of some fifty photographs at the national

AIA convention, followed by circulation to other cities. Competition photos selected for the AIA appointment calendar each year have made it a best-seller. Fuller continued to coordinate the competition, one of the more labor-intensive committee assignments since it requires the viewing of thousands of slides, but with rewards of national visibility for the St. Louis Chapter. Distinguished photographers and critics who have served as judges include Balthazar Korab, Timothy Hursley, E. Fay Jones, John Morris Dixon, and Cervin Robinson.

To recognize extraordinary career achievements by members, the Chapter created the St. Louis AIA Gold Honor

Award, first conferred on Joseph D. Murphy in 1983. Gerhardt Kramer received the award in 1987, and George Hellmuth in 1990. Kramer also received the George I. Barnett Award for distinguished service to the profession and the public from the Missouri Council of Architects at its 1985 meeting in the renovated Union Station.

Awards for individual projects had been instituted in the 1950s as design incentives and as recurring notice to the public of AIA emphasis on quality. This grew into a program of triennial awards to recognize excellence in three categories, with sponsorship by the Chapter and the Construction Products Council. The supplementary Interior Architecture Awards Program was organized by Dennis A. Cassani in 1984, with entries judged by the Houston AIA Chapter. The program was repeated in 1987, with Grace C. Corbin as chairperson, in connection with the meeting of the national AIA Interior Architecture Committee in St. Louis. In the next year the first Unbuilt Buildings Competition was organized by Philip J. Holden and judged by the Kansas City AIA Chapter. These three awards programs are now alternated annually, allowing all types of projects to be recognized—including meritorious designs that remain on paper.

Givens Hall revisited: The five deans of the Washington University School of Architecture since 1949, all on campus for the school's seventy-fifth anniversary in 1986, assembled at the front steps for a documentary photograph.

From left: Joseph D. Murphy, dean 1949-1952; Joseph Passonneau, 1956-1967; Constantine E. Michaelides, the dean since 1973; Buford Pickens, 1953-1956; and George Anselevicius, 1968-1973.

18
Convention City / Urban Transformation: 1989

For the fourth time in the Chapter's century, St. Louis was designated for the Institute's annual convention, in 1989, and as had happened previously, preconvention planning made bigger Chapter office space necessary. In 1986 under president Randall B. Miltenberger, the search by president-elect Thomas H. Teasdale and a task force led to a mezzanine suite in the historic Lammert Building at Washington Avenue and Tenth Street, a handsome Renaissance Revival building of 1897 by Eames & Young. After long service as a retail store for fine furniture, the building had just been remodeled for offices by Mackey & Associates.

The larger quarters allowed for an ample reception desk, a private executive vice-president's office for Betty Lou Custer, increased bookstore space for manager Vanessa Shriver, a new computer, and an urgently needed conference room with exhibition space and shelving for a reference library. Lawrence M. Malcic, Anthony M. DeMichele, and Eugene Mackey supervised the design, which incorporated architectural fragments—the doorway lintel stone of the old Architectural Club embellishes entry casework, and two terra-cotta ornaments salvaged from Louis Sullivan's demolished Garrick Theater in Chicago accent the conference room entrances. The relocation was completed in December 1986.

To help members of the growing Chapter become better acquainted, Karl Pettit scheduled monthly Firm Profile Tours—office open-house occasions for colleagues inaugurated by Holden Architects, Henderson Group, Lawrence Group, Inc., and Gilmore Malcic & Cannon. A peer review panel initiated by David Pearce encouraged member firms to improve their quality of practice by means of a structured review process.

Topics of workshops and seminars leaned toward technical matters increasingly a part of the architect's expertise—computers and computer-aided design (CAD) software, smart buildings, indoor pollution, building code revisions, contract changes, affordable housing—and they likewise figured in convention agendas.

Convention steering committee, 1989 (some not present): Along upper stair rail, in line to wall: Vanessa Shriver, William W. Stewart, Gregory S. Palermo, Bernice Roemer, Doris Ittner, Laurie Sperling, Chapter President Eugene J. Mackey III, and John Reeve. Back row, upper steps and landing: Cindy Petzoldt, Daniel Jay, Milton Bischof, Fred Powers, Dean Constantine Michaelides, Chester Roemer, Charles Danna, William Rupe, Randall Miltenberger, H. Curtis Ittner, and Karl Pettit. Lower steps and landing, clockwise spiral: Doris Danna (7 o'clock), Jane Wilhelms, Betty Lou Custer, Lawrence M. Malcic, George Nikolajevich (12 o'clock), Anthony M. DeMichele, Donald Porter Wilson, Carol Wilson, Norma Rupe, Fred DeWeese (5 o'clock), Ann Schwetye, Gay DeMichele, and Clark Davis.

The Chapter's hosting of another national convention depended on downtown hotel space for the expected 6,000 delegates, and completion of the Adam's Mark filled the quota. Sessions were scheduled at the Cervantes Convention Center.

H. Curtis Ittner, nearing the end of his term as president in 1985, was made chairman of planning. His seventeen-member steering committee met monthly for two years, then weekly during the final year of preparations. Like Ittner, seven of this group had been intensively involved in the 1964 St. Louis convention. Its members: Rex Becker, James Biehle, Betty Lou Custer, Charles Danna, Doris Danna, Clark Davis, Anthony DeMichele, Robert Elkington, Gale Hill, Doris Ittner, Eugene Mackey III, Lawrence Malcic, Constantine Michaelides, Randall Miltenberger, Gregory Palermo, Laurie

H. Curtis Ittner, 1989 convention chair, with his wife, Doris, who served on his committee. (Both had been active also in the 1964 convention.) Ittner, the 1985 Chapter president, is the son and grandson of previous presidents. He coordinated this Chapter history.

Sperling, and Thomas Teasdale.

Twenty-five years of downtown rejuvenation, including a construction boom in the mid-1980s, insured that visitors would see a transformed St. Louis, for which they would need a transformed AIA guidebook. Philip Cotton was chairman of the guidebook committee, and Doris Danna the project coordinator. George McCue, author of three editions of *The Building Art in St. Louis: Two Centuries,* and Frank Peters, retired arts editor and architecture critic of the *Post-Dispatch,* jointly wrote the text, and Pat Hays Baer drew the maps. Published by the University of Missouri Press, *A Guide to the Architecture of St. Louis* was distributed to convention delegates with their registration material, following a cliff-hanger delay because of a dock strike in Japan (where it was

printed). It is sold in bookstores.

The planning of events assured exposure of the city's attractions to the full extent of delegates' time and vitality. The VIP party, in the Ralston Purina headquarters garden, was organized by Donald Porter Wilson and his wife, Carol; Karl Pettit coordinated tours of the metropolitan area conducted mostly by Chapter members. Entertainment, notably St. Louis Symphony concerts on Saturday and Sunday nights, was organized by Anthony and Gay DeMichele. The first-night Host Chapter party for 1,278, a dinner cruise aboard the steamboat *President,* was planned by Chester Roemer and William Rupe. WAL members arranged tours for delegate spouses, with a breakfast at Missouri Botanical Garden and visits to private and museum houses. The WAL also managed the gift shop and hospitality lounge, and served 8,400 cookies and thousands of cups of coffee. In an event entitled Architectural Awareness in Schools, children assembled a nine-foot model of the Gateway Arch in a program, ''I Built the Arch,'' dealing with its history.

Architecture-related exhibits on view at several downtown galleries notably included ''The Exceptional One: Women in Architecture 1888-1988,'' at the Design Center, organized by the AIA Women in Architecture as a traveling show. It commemorated women's accomplishments in practice and theory, and the election of the first woman, Louise Blanchard Bethune, to the American Institute of Architects. To more than eighty items in the exhibition, the WIA added drawings by women architects of the St. Louis area, and produced a seven-minute video by Webster University's Kathy Corley with

Arteaga Photos, AIA Chapter Collection

Frank Peters and George McCue, coauthors of the 1989 convention guidebook, A Guide to the Architecture of St. Louis, *with Doris Danna, project coordinator.*

interviews. The WIA also sponsored a women's breakfast and showed films by Ray Eames.

"Five Choose Five" was the title of the Chapter-sponsored exhibition of work by five architects selected by five other prominent architects enlisted by Don Canty, an honorary member of the AIA and then editor of *Architecture* magazine. Other galleries showed perspective renderings by Steve Oles, paper columns designed by St. Louis artists and architects, and the Gateway Arch under construction. The St. Louis Public Library exhibited its collection of Louis Sullivan's drawings of the Wainwright Tomb.

The St. Louis public was not left in doubt about the architects' presence. Banners incorporating an ornamental motif from the Wainwright Building were

mounted on downtown streetlight standards, and convention leaders were interviewed on radio and television. The *Post-Dispatch* published fourteen articles about the convention, most of them by the newspaper's architecture critic, E. F. Porter, Jr.

These included prominent coverage of the AIA endorsement of preservation of the Eames & Young Cupples Station warehouses. The 1894-1917 complex, built with railroad tracks to interior loading docks and with other facilities for rapid transfer of freight, was hailed in its time as revolutionary technology and is recognized as superlative industrial architecture, particularly for its harmonious proportions and brick detailing. It is now owned by Washington University.

When the Cupples site near Busch

139 | Convention City

Eugene J. Mackey III, newly installed chapter president, is congratulated by his predecessor, Clark Davis, after the ceremony in December 1988, conducted by George Hellmuth, center.

Memorial Stadium was considered as a parking lot for a hockey arena, the university offered to sell if the city would issue a demolition permit. The architectural and preservation community rallied in protest, and president Eugene Mackey led the Chapter in its own resolution. Mayor Vincent C. Schoemehl, Jr. courageously halted the sale and called for a study to recycle the St. Louis landmark. He has since signed ordinances to establish a tax increment financing plan for the area.

Noting the lack of a St. Louis marker to commemorate Eero Saarinen and his career, the Chapter proposed a bronze plaque beneath the Gateway Arch on Leonor K. Sullivan Boulevard. Saarinen's son, Eric, and daughter, Susan, attended the dedication ceremony on May 7, 1989, sponsored jointly by the Institute and the Chapter. Again, there was an anxious wait, this time for the plaque, but it was delivered at the last minute. It was Eric's

first visit to the arch. The next year, the Gateway Arch was saluted again with the Institute's Twenty-five Year Award, its highest honor to a work of architecture at least a quarter-century old.

Later in that eventful year of Mackey's presidency, he arranged for a series of breakfast meetings that brought Chapter members and civic leaders together for discussions of mutual concerns. At a meeting in July Mayor Schoemehl attended with Christopher Grace, an urban design and development specialist from Boston who had just been employed by the city as economic director. Grace's appointment was followed by a better-informed approach to St. Louis planning, and his selection of Donald Royse as director of urban design (a newly created position) began a new era of professionalism in what had been a neglected area of concern. In 1990 Mayor Schoemehl was made an honorary member of the Institute.

Even as the convention was becoming history, architects were beginning to feel an economic pinch. Many firms found commissions falling off, and when the executive board asked for a dues increase in 1989 and 1990, both elections rejected it by slim margins. The Chapter adjusted its activities to include free or low-cost programs, such as a ''Tough Times Soup Supper'' catered by the WAL for both AIA and nonmember architects to discuss survival strategies.

The Chapter trimmed its budgets, cut back on the *Newsletter,* and tried creative fund-raising to help finance its 1991 centennial celebration. Remembering a successful auction of architect-made birdhouses in 1988, Dan S. Mitchell and Andrew Trivers planned an auction of

In "I Built the Arch," an Architectural Awareness in Schools convention program, a youngster puts a summit section into a nine-foot model of the Gateway Arch with steadying by Walter Kromm.

architect-made garden ornaments for 1990. It raised more than $7,500 to benefit the St. Louis Foundation for Architecture.

The celebration of the Chapter's first hundred years had to be planned under the same budget limitations, but the Chapter resolved to make it memorable with planning led by president-elect Fred A. Powers for the year's events. He enlisted Curtis Ittner as coordinator of the Chapter's history, with Doris Danna, Vickie L. Berry, and Andrew Gunn helping to collect archival materials. Robert Elkington, Frederick Sternberg, and Charles Danna contacted senior Chapter members and community leaders to record their recollections.

The first event was a January luncheon in tribute to Howard Baer for civic leadership, particularly for his support of high standards in architecture. The main public events were two exhibitions. Scheduled for September 1991 through March 1992 in the Missouri Historical Society's main gallery was "The Architect's Mark: a Century of St. Louis Architectural Drawings," organized by Fred E. DeWeese, Jeffrey L. Blydenburgh, and the MHS staff. It brought together concept sketches, presentation drawings, working drawings, travel notes, and other work in many

Tim Parker

Behind every event there is a committee, such as the Spirit of '91 team that created the Centennial celebration. Top row: Michael Blaes, Andrew Gunn, and Albert B. Fuller. Fourth row: William Rupe, Richard Henmi, William Bodley Lane; Frederick Sternberg, and Richard Bliss. Third row: Charles Danna, Vickie Berry, *Andrew Trivers, and Jeffrey Blydenburgh. Second row: Fred DeWeese, authors Esley Hamilton, George McCue, and Carolyn Hewes Toft (Mary Henderson Gass was not present). Front row: Chester Roemer, Eugene J. Mackey III, President-elect Doris Danna, and President Fred Powers.*

media and techniques—the work of many hands and minds. The other exhibition, at the St. Louis Art Museum, was a display of the Cass Gilbert watercolor renderings of the building that was the permanent unit of the World's Fair Art Palace. Robert E. Entzeroth was consultant for the Gilbert exhibition.

The Chapter's culminating celebration was the Gala Party organized by Chester

Roemer and William Rupe, concluding the Chapter's observance of a landmark year with installation of Doris Danna, the first woman to serve as its president.

In February of the Centennial Year, Betty Lou Custer, the Chapter's executive vice-president, died of cancer. In her years of service, beginning as a member of the Chapter and of the Women's Architectural

Fred Powers, president 1991 and chairman of the Centennial Steering Committee.

League, she served first as unstinting worker on many projects and then, since 1972, as executive secretary and finally as executive vice-president. Betty Lou shaped and disciplined the organization with dedication that would be impossible to match.

As a young member, she was a constant source of ideas, one innovation being her column, ''Et Cetera . . . BLC'' in the early 1960s for *Construction News and Review.* In 1988, when the *Newsletter* was redesigned, she revived her column after a ten-year hiatus. She wrote, ''With a membership of almost 650, with more than twenty committees and groups that meet regularly, there is more news than space will accommodate. Here is the place for the smaller, more personal items, of somewhat human interest.'' Indeed, her columns were invariably packed with information, and if anthologized would serve as an informal history of Chapter activities during her career. The Et Cetera column will continue to be a *Newsletter* feature.

The BLC writing style was as individual as the hair band that she was never seen without—direct, slightly breathless, always enthusiastic, full of superlatives and pronouncements. ''Instead of April showers, April gave us meetings, meetings, and more meetings. . . . Highlight of the NYC/AIA convention was our super St.

Katherine Hoester (right), who as executive director manages the AIA Chapter office with Patricia Bausch, associate director. Both took office at a full run in the midst of Centennial planning with an erratic computer.

Louis group . . . The 1989 Calendars are now available and are gorgeous! . . . Racquet Club food is second to none. Not to be missed.'' On the other hand, she could be the stern, tough den mother: ''A word of caution to several SL/AIA—have you paid your dues to national—notices were sent with warnings of termination. Of all the times in your career—now is the time to be an active member of your professional organization.''

As the Chapter reflects on its past and ponders its future, Betty Lou Custer will be sadly missed.

Betty Lou Custer receiving an award plaque from President Kenneth M. Schaefer in 1970 for her creation of Architects' Sunday, the Chapter's most successful effort to generate public concern with architecture. Betty Lou Custer, FAIA, managed the program until her death in February 1991.

Appendix

Presidents of the St. Louis Chapter, AIA

Until 1964, Chapter presidents served from July to June, and the terms for that period are designated by the year of installation. Beginning with 1964, the terms have been by the calendar year and are designated by the year of service.

First Charter 1884
Henry G. Isaacs

Second Charter
1890	P. P. Furber/
	William S. Eames
1891	William S. Eames
1892	Thomas C. Young
1893	Thomas C. Young
1894	Thomas B. Annan
1895	Robert W. Walsh
1896	Charles K. Ramsey
1897	Charles K. Ramsey
1898	Thomas C. Young
1899	William B. Ittner
1900	William B. Ittner
1901	William S. Eames
1902	John L. Mauran
1903	John L. Mauran
1904	Theodore C. Link
1905	Theodore C. Link
1906	Ernest J. Russell
1907	William S. Eames
1908	William S. Eames
1909	Thomas C. Young
1910	Thomas C. Young
1911	Ernest C. Klipstein
1912	Ernest C. Klipstein
1913	George F. Brueggemann
1914	George F. Brueggemann
1915	Ernest J. Russell
1916	Ernest J. Russell
1917	Montrose P. McArdle
1918	Louis LaBeaume
1920	Louis LaBeaume
1921	Walter L. Rathmann

1922	Walter L. Rathmann
1923	William A. Hirsch
1924	William A. Hirsch
1925	James P. Jamieson
1926	James P. Jamieson
1927	L. Baylor Pendleton
1928	L. Baylor Pendleton
1929	Wilbur T. Trueblood
1930	Wilbur T. Trueblood
1931	Eugene S. Kline
1932	Eugene S. Kline
1933	W. Oscar Mullgardt
1934	W. Oscar Mullgardt
1935	P. John Hoener
1936	P. John Hoener
1937	Benedict Farrar
1938	Benedict Farrar
1939	George W. Spearl
1940	George W. Spearl
1941	William B. Ittner, Jr.
1942	Lawrence Hill
1943	Lawrence Hill
1944	Fred R. Hammond
1945	Fred R. Hammond
1946	William B. Ittner, Jr.
1947	Kenneth E. Wischmeyer
1948	Kenneth E. Wischmeyer
1949	Arthur E. Koelle
1950	Arthur E. Koelle
1951	Joseph D. Murphy
1952	William A. Grolock
1953	Lester C. Haeckel
1954	Robert Elkington
1955	Arthur Schwarz
1956	Rex L. Becker
1957	Eugene J. Mackey, Jr.

1958	Gerhardt Kramer
1959	Frederick C. Sternberg
1960	Harris Armstrong
1961	John David Sweeney
1962	John David Sweeney
1963	John David Sweeney
1964	George E. Kassabaum
1965	George E. Kassabaum
1966	Angelo G. Corrubia
1967	Angelo G. Corrubia
1968	Nolan L. Stinson, Jr.
1969	Nolan L. Stinson, Jr.
1970	Kenneth M. Schaefer
1971	Theodor Mann Hoener
1972	Chester E. Roemer
1973	D. Robert Downey
1974	Joseph A. Cernik
1975	Bryce Hastings
1976	William W. Rupe
1977	Thomas M. Tebbetts
1978	Charles Danna
1979	Laurance P. Berri
1980	William M. Pistrui
1981	Anthony M. DeMichele
1982	Robert G. Galloway
1983	Albert B. Fuller, Jr.
1984	Gregory S. Palermo
1985	H. Curtis Ittner
1986	Randall B. Miltenberger
1987	Thomas H. Teasdale
1988	Clark S. Davis
1989	Eugene J. Mackey, III
1990	Eugene J. Mackey, III
1991	Fred A. Powers
1992	Doris Andrews Danna

St. Louis Chapter
Fellows of the
American Institute of Architects

1890	Thomas C. Young	1952	Lawrence Hill	1970	Gerhardt Kramer
1891	Ernst C. Janssen	1955	Harris Armstrong	1972	Betty Lou Custer
1891	William B. Ittner, Sr.	1957	Joseph D. Murphy	1973	George F. Hellmuth
1894	Robert W. Walsh	1959	Kenneth E. Wischmeyer	1974	Robert E. Entzeroth
1902	John Lawrence Mauran	1964	Eugene J. Mackey, Jr.	1975	Verner I. Burks, Jr.
1906	James P. Jamieson	1964	Joseph Passonneau	1976	Kenneth M. Schaefer
1909	Ernest J. Russell	1964	Eric W. Smith, Jr.	1977	Richard L. Bliss
1941	Ernest C. Klipstein	1964	Hari Van Hoefen	1980	Thomas H. Teasdale
1915	George F. A. Brueggeman	1965	Robert Elkington	1982	William A. Bernoudy
1923	Louis LaBeaume	1966	John David Sweeney	1983	Constantine E. Michaelides
1925	Walter L. Rathmann	1967	Rex L. Becker	1985	William Bowersox
1934	Wilbur T. Trueblood	1967	George E. Kassabaum	1989	Albert B. Fuller, Jr.
1938	Eugene S. Kline	1967	Charles E. King	1989	Gregory S. Palermo
1940	Guy Study	1967	Buford L. Pickens	1990	H. Curtis Ittner
1941	George W. Spearl	1969	Gyo Obata	1991	Eugene J. Mackey, III
1944	W. Oscar Mullgardt				

St. Louis Chapter Members
Who Have Served the Institute

1889	Charles E. Illsley Director	1916	John L. Mauran President	1940	Benedict Farrar Director
1891	William S. Eames Director	1920	William B. Ittner Director	1942	Kenneth E. Wischmeyer Director
1892	Pierce P. Furber Director	1920	Ernest J. Russell Director	1949	Kenneth E. Wischmeyer Second Vice-president
1893	A. F. Rosenheim Director (appointed to fill Furber's unexpired term)	1922	Ernest J. Russell First Vice-president	1951	Kenneth E. Wischmeyer First Vice-president
1894	William S. Eames Second Vice-president	1924	William B. Ittner Treasurer	1965	George E. Kassabaum Vice-president
1894	Theodore C. Link Director	1929	Louis LaBeaume Director	1966	Rex L. Becker Director
1899	William S. Eames First Vice-president	1930	Ernest J. Russell First Vice-president	1967	George E. Kassabaum First Vice-president
1904	William S. Eames President	1932	Ernest J. Russell President	1968	George E. Kassabaum President
1906	John L. Mauran Director	1934	Ernest J. Russell President	1969	Rex L. Becker Treasurer
1914	John L. Mauran Treasurer	1936	Louis LaBeaume Vice-president	1977	Thomas H. Teasdale Director

1977	George E. Kassabaum	1986	Gregory S. Palermo	1990	Thomas H. Teasdale
	Chancellor, College of Fellows		Director		Bursar, College of Fellows
1980	Thomas H. Teasdale	1989	Gregory S. Palermo		
	Vice-president		Vice-president		

Award Recipients

St. Louis Chapter Gold Honor Award

1983   Joseph D. Murphy
1987   Gerhardt Kramer
1990   George F. Hellmuth

George I. Barnett Award

1980   Thomas H. Teasdale
1983   Joseph A. Cernik
1985   Gerhardt Kramer

Missouri Council of Architects
Architect of the Year Award

1976   David W. Pearce
1978   George E. Kassabaum

Distinguished Service Award

1988   H. Curtis Ittner

St. Louis Chapter Members
Who Have Served the State Organization

Missouri State Association
of Registered Architects

1954   Rex L. Becker
      Secretary

1960   John David Sweeney
      President

1961   David W. Pearce
      President

1962   David W. Pearce
      President

1964   Edward J. Thias
      President

Missouri Association of Registered Architects

1965   Edward J. Thias
      President

1968   Gerhardt Kramer
      Secretary

1970   Gerhardt Kramer
      Secretary

Missouri Council of Architects

1972   Gerhardt Kramer
      President-elect

1973   Gerhardt Kramer
      President

1974   David W. Pearce
      President-elect

1975   David W. Pearce
      President

1976   Thomas E. Phillips
      (Cape Girardeau)
      Secretary

1977   William P. McMahon
      President-elect

1978   William P. McMahon
      President

1978   William W. Rupe
      Secretary

1979   Theodor Mann Hoener
      (Cape Girardeau)
      Secretary

1979   Walter B. Kromm
      Treasurer

1980   Walter B. Kromm
      President-elect

1981   Walter B. Kromm
      President

1981   Gale A. Hill
      Treasurer

1982   Fred DeWeese
      Treasurer

1983   C. Robert Stearnes (Sikeston)
      Secretary

1983   Robert L. Praprotnik
      Treasurer

1984   Robert L. Praprotnik
      President-elect

1985   Robert L. Praprotnik
      President

1985   Peter H. Green
      Treasurer

1986	Peter H. Green Secretary	
1986	Don A. Walters Treasurer	
1987	Dan S. Mitchell Treasurer	
1988	Dan S. Mitchell President-elect	

1988	John Hoelscher Treasurer
1989	Dan S. Mitchell President
1989	Vickie L. Berry Treasurer

1991	William Yarger President-elect
1991	Mary Ann Lazarus Treasurer
1992	William Yarger President

Presidents of the Women's Architectural League of St. Louis

1960	Louise Armstrong	1971	Harriet Lickhalter	1982	Audrey Berri
1961	Edith Kiewitt	1972	Florine Sorkin	1983	Linda DeWeese
1962	Ada Becker	1973	Mary Lou Drosten	1984	Elaine Ohlhausen
1963	Bee Freeman	1974	Rosemary Field	1985	Norma Deen Jura'csik
1964	Micki Smith	1975	Olive Cernik	1986	Dolores Hill
1965	Bernice Roemer	1976	Judith Hoffmann	1987	Sherry Turner
1966	Norma Rupe	1977	Susan Galloway	1988	Doris Danna
1967	Kayo Stinson	1978	Mary Ann Fuller	1989	Doris Danna
1968	Doris Danna	1979	Pat Schneeberger	1990	Ann Schwetye
1969	Minne Grunik	1980	Gay DeMichele	1991	Ann Schwetye
1970	Patricia Hastings	1981	Jane Wilhelms	1992	Jacqueline Ruthsatz

Presidents of St. Louis Architectural Club

1894	J. Willard Adams	1905	John C. Stephens	1917	Angelo B. M. Corrubia
1895	Oscar Enders	1906	Wilbur T. Trueblood	1918	Frank M. F. Cann
1896	J. W. Ginder	1907	Albert D. Millar	1918	H. H. H. Lynch
1897	Wm. B. Ittner	1907	Eugene L. Pleitsch	1919	H. H. H. Lynch
1898	Wm. B. Ittner	1908	Henry S. Pitts	1920	W. Oscar Mullgardt
1899	R. M. Milligan	1909	Eugene S. Klein	1921	H. H. H. Lynch
1900	Edward Gordon Garden	1910	Alfred M. Lane	1922	F. Ray Leimkuehler
1901	Geo. F. A. Brueggeman	1911	John J. Roch	1923	Clemens Nicholas
1902	Charles O. Pfeil	1912	David Stephen, Jr.	1924	John A. Bryan
1902	John C. Stephens	1913	W. Oscar Mullgardt	1925	Daniel J. Carroll
1903	Ernest Helfensteller	1914	Hugo K. Graf	1926	Alfred H. Norrish
1904	Jesse N. Watson	1915	Norman I. Bailey	1927	John A. Bryan
		1916	Edward C. Christopher		

Honorary Members, AIA

1873 James B. Eads	1925 George F. Steedman	1983 William E. Maritz
1893 Halsey C. Ives	1927 Samuel L. Sherer	1984 Leon Strauss
1894 J. B. Johnson	1960 Mayor Raymond R. Tucker	1989 Carolyn Hewes Toft
1895 Julius Pitzman	1964 George McCue	1991 Mayor Vincent C. Schoemehl

Honorary Associates, St. Louis Chapter, AIA

1927 Holmes Smith	1957 George E. Mylonas	1979 Martha Scharff Hilligoss
1931 Harland Bartholomew	1959 Charles van Ravenswaay	1981 Bill Pautler
1943 Emil Frei, Jr.	1961 Walter R. Crecelius	1982 Martin P. Walsh, Jr.
1950 Perry T. Rathbone	1964 Kenneth Hudson	1983 Jane E. Piper
1952 Albert Baum	1969 Dorothy B. Neuman	1983 Marion Piper
1952 Alfred Roth	1974 Austin P. Leland	1983 Vernon W. Piper
1957 Fred E. Conway	1979 Kathie Davis	1987 Harriet Rodes Bakewell

Contributors

St. Louis Chapter, AIA Firms

Kenneth Balk & Associates, Inc.
The Benham Group, Inc.
Burks Associates
Cannon St. Louis, Inc.
Jamie Cannon Associates, Inc.
The Christner Partnership, Inc.
Patrick Croghan & Associates, Inc.
Robert Elkington, FAIA, Architect
    and Consultant
Earl A. Fey, AIA
Michael Fox, Inc.
Robert Galloway, Architects, Inc.
Mary Henderson Gass, Architect
Gruchalla & Cover Architects
Hastings & Chivetta Architects
Hellmuth, Obata & Kassabaum,
    Inc.
The Hoffmann Group P.C.
The Hoffmann Partnership, Inc.
Horner & Shifrin, Inc.
Interior Space, Inc.

Ittner & Bowersox, Inc.
Kromm, Rikimaru & Johansen, Inc.
Kuhlmann Design Group, Inc.
Harold L. LePere and Associates
    Inc.
Harry C. LePique, Architect
Mackey Associates, P.C.
Raymond E. Maritz and Sons, Inc.
Paul Marti Associates, Architects
Murphy, Downey, Wofford &
    Richman
Peckham Guyton Albers & Viets
Powers Associates, Inc.
Stone, Marraccini & Patterson
Sverdrup Corporation
Wedemeyer, Cernik, Corrubia, Inc.
P. H. Weis & Associates, Inc.
The Wind Architectural Group
The Wischmeyer Architects
Yarger Associates

St. Louis Chapter, AIA Members

Matt C. Adams, AIA	James W. Alverson, AIA	Laura Neri Baebler, AIA
William H. Albinson, AIA	David A. Anderson, AIA	W. Marion Bamman, AIA

Rex L. Becker, FAIA
Lisa Bell-Reim, Associate
Laurance P. Berri, AIA
Donald J. Berry, AIA
Paul M. Berry, AIA
Vickie L. Berry, AIA
Rudolph Beuc, Jr., AIA
James T. Biehle, AIA
Milton J. Bischof, Jr., AIA
Richard L. Bliss, FAIA
Jeffrey L. Blydenburgh, AIA
Larry D. Brocaw, AIA
D. Gregory Brown, AIA
Joseph Burzinski, AIA
Thomas H. Cahoon, AIA
Paul Scott Cameron, AIA
Joseph A. Cernik, AIA
Bernard W. Colton, AIA
Harold Colton, Professional Affiliate
Grace C. Corbin, AIA
Angelo G. Corrubia, AIA
W. Philip Cotton, Jr., AIA
D. Eugene Coughlin, AIA
Patrick R. Croghan, AIA
Charles Danna, AIA
Doris Andrews Danna, AIA
Clark S. Davis, AIA
Gary R. Dedeke, AIA
Anthony M. DeMichele, AIA
Fred E. DeWeese, AIA
Helen Kessler DiFate, AIA
Raymond F. Donohue, AIA
D. Robert Downey, AIA
Mary Lou Drosten,
    Professional Affiliate
Paul F. Duell, AIA
Mark Duitsman, AIA
Cynthia S. Easterling, AIA
Ruth V. Eckart, AIA
Ronald R. Edwards, AIA
Peter W. Fairchild, AIA
Steven M. Feeler, AIA
Adolph Felder, AIA
Merrick Felder, AIA
Stephanie Felder-Naor, Associate
Earl A. Fey, AIA
Stephen C. Fichet, AIA
Harry A. Fine, AIA
Dorothy J. Fleming on behalf of the
    late Eugene H. Fleming, AIA
Don M. Foster, AIA
Michael Fox, Professional Affiliate
Albert B. Fuller, Jr., FAIA

Ronald G. Galemore, AIA
Mary Henderson Gass, AIA
Glenn Gauger, AIA
Ronald K. Gilmore, AIA
Marvin A. Ginsberg, AIA
Jane H. Godfrey, AIA
Gary R. Goldberg, AIA
King Graf, AIA
Marjory K. Graff on behalf of the
    late George E. Kassabaum, FAIA
Carolyn Green, Associate
J. Robert Green, AIA
Frank J. Gruchalla, AIA
John C. Guenther, AIA
Andrew Gunn, AIA
Karl Eidson Guyer, AIA
James L. Haack, AIA
Goerge B. Hagee, AIA
Ireneus Harasymiak, AIA
Edward M. Heine, AIA
Gale A. Hill, AIA
Frederick W. Hill, AIA
Robert A. Hill, AIA
Billie Hirsch on behalf of the late
    Oliver B. Hirsch, AIA
John B. Hoag, IV, AIA
Katherine Hoester,
    Executive Director
Joseph G. Hoffmann, AIA
Judith Hoffmann on behalf of the
    late David L. Hoffmann, AIA
Philip J. Holden, AIA
Stephen J. Hollander, AIA
Jomes M. Holtzman, AIA
Donald G. Hussman, AIA
H. Curtis Ittner, FAIA
Theodore R. Jacobs, AIA
Daniel G. Jay, AIA
Maurice C. Johansen, AIA
Jane Hall Johnson, AIA
John E. Jones, AIA
Charles F. Jost, AIA
Curt C. Juergens, AIA
Douglas F. Julien, AIA
Klaus H. Kattentidt, AIA
Raynard 0. Kearbey, AIA
Linda S. Kenney, Associate
Charles E. King, FAIA
Richard B. Kirschner, AIA
Erwin W. H. Knoesel, AIA
Gerhardt Kramer, FAIA
David V. Kromm, AIA
Young-Hie Nahm Kromm, AIA

Walter B. Kromm, AIA
Dennis E. Krost, AIA
Thom B. Kuntzman, AIA
Kwendeche, AIA
Kurt Landberg, AIA
Mary Ann Lazarus, AIA
Harold L. LePere, AIA
D. Anne Lewis,
    Professional Affiliate
Steven E. Lichtenfeld, AIA
Merlin E. Lickhalter, AIA
Chandan K. Mahanta, AIA
Lei-Hoo Mak, AIA
Lawrence M. Malcic, AIA
Louis Malin, AIA
Ferdinand H. Manger, II, AIA
William E. Manz, AIA
Raymond E. Maritz, AIA
Larry E. Marks, AIA
Paul E. Marti, Jr., AIA
Carl W. Martin, AIA
David P. Mastin, AIA
Arthur G. Matia, Associate
Oliver C. Matlock, AIA
Thomas 0. McCune, AIA
Bernard McMahon, AIA
Michael J. Meier, AIA
Constantine E. Michaelides, FAIA
Randall B. Miltenberger, AIA
Dan S. Mitchell, AIA
Larry B. More, AIA
Jeffrey P. Mugg, AIA
John R. Muldoon, AIA
Raymond E. Naughton, Jr., AIA
G. Dennie Neilson, AIA
Karl Nicoloff, AIA
Aaron D. Novack, AIA
Stuart L. Oberheu, AIA
William Odell, AIA
Edward J. Ortmann, AIA
Daniel R. Overmann, AIA
John F. Pahde, AIA
Bill Pautler,
    Honorary Associate SL/AIA
David W. Pearce, AIA
Lu Perantoni, Associate
Robert Pettus, Associate
John W. Pfaff, AIA
Thomas E. Phillips, AIA
Guy C. Picardi, AIA
Marion Piper,
    Honorary Associate SL/AIA

Vernon W. Piper,
    Honorary Associate SL/AIA
William M. Pistrui, AIA
Gregory J. Polanik, AIA
Warren E. Poole, AIA
Fred A. Powers, AIA
Jerry Raeder, AIA
Andrew L. Raimist, Associate
Ronald M. Reim, AIA
Harry B. Richman, AIA
Chester E. Roemer, FAIA
Lester 0. Roth, AIA
Dale E. Ruthsatz, Associate
Pamela D. R. Rutledge, Associate
Philip W. Salembier, AIA
Janet Salmond, IBD
David L. Sanders, AIA
Denise Derickson Schaberg, AIA
William M. Schaberg, AIA
Kenneth M. Schaefer, FAIA
Edward A. Schilling, AIA
L. John Schott, AIA
Donald E. Schultz, AIA
Richard J. Schultz, AIA
Frederick S. Scott, AIA
Paul R. Sedovic, AIA
M. Glynn Shumake, AIA
Richard L. Siemons, AIA
Brad L. Simmons, AIA
Eric W. Smith, Jr., FAIA
Debra Smith-McClure, AIA
Marion B. Smith, AIA
Marvin L. Sokolik,
    Professional Affiliate
Jack Sorkin, AIA
R. Scott Starling, AIA
C. Robert Stearnes, AIA
Fred C. Sternberg, AIA
William W. Stewart, AIA
Leon R. Strauss, Honorary AIA
Paul E. Strohm, AIA
John R. Sturdevant, AIA
Judy C. Suhre, Associate
Ihtesham Ali Syed, Associate
James J. Syrett, AIA
Thomas H. Teasdale, FAIA
Thomas M. Tebbetts, AIA
Barry R. Thalden, AIA
Michael A. Thomas, AIA
Andrew Trivers, AIA
M. Kent Turner, AIA
Thomas A. Tyler, AIA

Stanley G. Urban, AIA
James Van Hook, Jr., AIA
Lawrence E. Viene, AIA
Reed I. Voorhees, AIA
Richard B. Wagner, Honorary
  Associate SL/AIA
Robert G. Watel, Jr., Associate

Janel Rothberg White, AIA
David W. Whiteman, AIA
Russell G. Wick, Jr., AIA
Gerald A. Wild, AIA
John B. Wildridge, AIA
Edward W. Wilhelms, AIA
Paul T. Wilhelms, AIA

Thomas W. Wilkins, AIA
Ronald R. Williams, AIA
Donald Porter Wilson, AIA
Kenneth E. Wischmeyer, FAIA
Theodore J. Wofford, AIA
James P. Woodworth, AIA
Heinz Zobel, AIA

Special Gifts

The American Institute of
  Architects/Kansas City Chapter,
  in memory of Betty Lou Custer,
  FAIA

Marcella T. and Dorothy T.
  Rinderer, in memory of Betty
  Lou Custer, FAIA

St. Louis Chapter AIA Scholarship Fund

James A. Singer

The Women's Architectural League
  of St. Louis in memory of Betty
  Lou Custer, FAIA

Acknowledgments

The authors of this book are deeply obligated to archivists Tony P. Wrenn and Kate Crandall, of the staff of the American Institute of Architects, Washington, for their patient searches for records of the St. Louis Chapter in Institute files, and for their accounting of the national activities of St. Louis members.

Pat Riner Amick, executive director of the Missouri Council of Architects, provided similar data on the state level, and registration records were checked by Shirley Nixon, executive director of the Missouri Board for Architects, Professional Engineers and Land Surveyors.

The many resources in the St. Louis Public Library were made available by Glen E. Holt, executive director; Jean E. Meeh Gosebrink, special collections librarian, and Mary S. Ens Frechette, manager of the Fine Arts Department. Charles Brown, librarian of the St. Louis Mercantile Library Association, opened his photographic files to a prolonged search for illustrations, as did Nancy Roenfeldt of the Finan Publishing Company. This project also drew on the archives of the Landmarks Association of St. Louis for information and illustrations.

Historians Frances Hurd Stadler and Nini Harris kindly read portions of the manuscript against notes in their materials.

During many times of need assistance was given by many members of the St. Louis Chapter AIA—more people than could be adequately thanked on this page. Betty Lou Custer, executive vice-president, was instrumental in the early organization of the project right to the time of her death, after which president-elect Doris Danna assisted with research and coordination. Gerhardt Kramer opened his extensive personal files to the researchers.

Others responded to special needs. Andrew Gunn and Vickie Berry helped in the inventory of Chapter archives; Robert Elkington and Frederick C. Sternberg interviewed senior Chapter members to clarify some uncertainties and to collect reminiscences; those who aided in interpretation of old minutes and in filling information gaps include Richard Bliss, Richard Henmi, Harry Richman, and Edward J. Thias.

H. Curtis Ittner supervised the book production. Scott Hueting of Hellmuth, Obata & Kassabaum provided valuable design expertise, and his firm generously allowed use of his time and HOK facilities. The book reflects the steadfast personal interest of Gregory M. Franzwa and Betty Burnett of The Patrice Press.

Each illustration is credited when sources are known, and the Chapter's thanks are extended to these sources for photographs and drawings, and for permission to reproduce them.

The Authors

Carolyn Hewes Toft has been executive director of Landmarks Association of St. Louis since 1978. She served previously as the historic preservation officer of the St. Louis Community Development Agency and taught at Washington University. Her book, *St. Louis: Landmarks & Historic Districts,* is in its third printing. She is the author and co-author of numerous Landmarks publications on St. Louis historic districts and architecture, and is an honorary member of the American Institute of Architects. This part of her career was preceded by several years of music study in this country and in Germany.

Esley Hamilton has been associated with the historic preservation efforts of the St. Louis County Department of Parks and Recreation since 1977, and during the same time has been adjunct instructor in Western architecture at Maryville College. He also has taught at Washington University and the University of Missouri-St. Louis and has served as historic preservation consultant for the cities of University City, Hannibal, and Clarksville, Missouri, and for Tower Grove Park. He is the author of *Historic Buildings in St. Louis County,* of a guide to Hannibal's historic buildings, and of numerous articles.

Mary Henderson Gass, AIA, is a St. Louis architect and principal of her own firm since 1988. A graduate of the Washington University School of Architecture, her writings include criticism and articles for *Inland Architect* on subjects in St. Louis and elsewhere. She is a member of the national AIA Committee on Design, and currently chairs the Historic Preservation Commission of University City.

George McCue was art and urban design critic for the *St. Louis Post-Dispatch* for nineteen years, and in retirement has written and edited books and catalogs on architecture and sculpture. He was the author of three editions of *The Building Art in St. Louis: Two Centuries,* and co-author of *A Guide to the Architecture of St. Louis,* all sponsored by the St. Louis Chapter, AIA, and *Sculpture City: St. Louis,* a history of the area's public sculpture sponsored by Laumeier Sculpture Park. He is an honorary member of the American Institute of Architects.

Index